JAZZ ZOOM carryin' it on

Photos and Interviews by Desdemone Bardin

DVC Press in association with Overtime Records, Inc.,

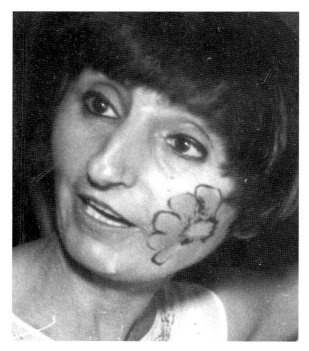

Desdemone Bardin (1928 - 2001)

May she rest in peace, bathed in the assurance of all the answers and the accomplishment of the desires that propelled her all her life. We wish during the coming years that those moments when she chooses to visit us will be ones of sweet epiphany.

INTRODUCTION

DESDEMONE: This book is a tribute to Jazz, American Classical music as many African American musicians call it. Here's where I'm coming from. Back in the days while listening to the radio in Paris, I heard a song that really blew my mind - it was Bessie Smith. I was 12 years old, still there was no doubt in my mind: "This was My music!" Bewitched, addicted, call it what you like, I was hooked and became a fervent Jazz agitproptiste, doing battle for the cause at every opportunity.

We'd be in the clubs of St. Germain des Pres, or elsewhere, dancing like crazy...breaking out, rebels without a pause...reaching for higher ground. For us, the music said it all, BODY AND SOUL.

So I say, "Carry it on!" Just recently, I heard someone in New York say, "Jazz is dead!" I told him, "Bullshit!" This music is an idiom unto itself. It has unstoppable strength, boundless creativity - the wild improvisations, the irresistible humor - and steadfast artists." Get the facts! Read what they say in Jazz Zoom.

I want to particularly thank the great violinist, Leroy Jenkins, who encouraged me to get this project done so that those who have played futuristic music these many years will not be forgotten during their lifetimes.

Photo - James Spady

Bright Moments. Dark Phases. The Rhythm and The Blues. The BeBop and The Hip Hop of it all. Gospelations. Negro Folksongs. The Blues. Trane. Murray. Billie. Lee. Duke. Papa Joe. Philly Jo. Musiq. Body and Soul. The Prez and The Lady. Day and Night. Memories. Motions. Music. Bessie and Son House. Boats crossing the Atlantic. Dessalines crossing Napoleon. Wayblackmemories this bright sunny Sunday in St. Denis. And all you could hear was Musiq coming from Braxton's Tri-Centric Orchestra. Light and Dark. Young and strong. Running against the wind. Take three. Odd meters. Twisted sound coming from the Underground of Bruknawmnnnnnnnnnn. Break. These are the breaks. Holy Midnights sing Eve. Sun Ra takes the A train. Bardin riding New Lots Express. Both moving fast.

It is the hue-manity and Africanite that lifts these images off the page, elevates them in some home/field. This photographer is familiar with the subjects of her camera's eye. All seeing Third and Ninth eyes. Randy Weston smiles knowingly as he prepares for prayer. Wynton Kelley hears the muted sound of a broken robin. Traci knows the deep Garvey spirit lives. It is midday in Brooklyn. Nightfalls in Chelsea. Spoken words speaking in tongues. And what can one say of the magnificent representation of Abbey Lincoln representin': "It was very long ago but I remember still/the house with many many rooms that stood upon a hill." Zooming deep into the black holes where these musicians be. Behind the camera. Outside of the range of the gaze. Living just enough for the cité. 50 Cents meets Les Nubians. Between the covered particularities one can see/hear Jackie McLean's swift move from Jonathan to Sun Ra and Charlie Parker. Bird Lives in Desdemone Bardin's spirit motions, her dark phases and trusting eyes. She lives in the margins of each image because if you know her you'll know she has a story locked into each photograph.

Rhythms and Sounds

One Tuesday morning I received a call from Paris, France. It was the distinctive voice of the remarkable French photographer, sociolinguist, hiphopographer and raconteur Dr. Desdemone Bardin. We reconnected after many years of silence. St. Denis to Paris to Harlem. She was the scholar on Black music who pioneered in using rap lyrics to teach English to native French users eager to learn this thing called Américan English and Desse knew that the golden key lies in Ebonics. Bardin introduced Nouvelle Poésie Black Americaine into her classes at Université Paris 8 , Vincennes à St. Denis. Who else but Desdemone Bardin could have une grande présentation multimedia of Rhythms and Sounds (in conjunction with UFR ARTS) to celebrate the 25th anniversary of the Univesité Paris 8. Yes!!!! Yeahhhhhhhhhhhhhhhhh!!! So eclectic is her taste that she sees the commonalties in Brother Blue, Martin Luther King, Jr., Spike Lee, Public Enemy , Malcolm X and Andrew Cyrille. That's how Hip She Be when she Be Bops. Scatting her way into the black and blue world of existentialism.

Jazz and Hip Hop Recombinations

Memories carry me back to evidence of her enthusiasm about the first book in our trilogy on Rap Music and Hip Hop Culture, Nation Conscious Rap. It was the overwhelming response of my French compatriots Olivier Cachin, Bernard Zekri, David Dufresne, Pierre Monod, Francois Ndong, Desdemone Bardin and Andre Prevos, that formed an unbreakable link to the Francophone Hip Hop Community. Although Desse often told me how much Nation Conscious Rap influenced her still neglected book, Free Style and I would respond by telling her 'but we didn't have those slamming Grafs, Pieces, Space images up in there. She is the one who challenged Jazz musicians visiting France to declare where they stood on Hip Hop artistry and to actually be in conversation with Hip Hop Artists. Her son, Sebastian, is the end result of all of that Great Black Music running from the Seine to the Mississippi, from Marseille and Toulouse to Philly and Brooklyn. Spirits Rejoice/Rejoins those African voices. Woeeeeeeeeee. I said, Woeeeeeeeeeeeeeeeeeeeeeeeeeeeeeeeeeee!!! Sound explosions all up in that Jazz Boom Zoom. JBZ. Desse knows what she's doing. She planned all of this. She knew they'd finally catch up with her vision.

M. Maurice Cullaz, the noted Jazz lover puts it in the side pocket when he says, " I congratulate Desdemone Bardin , a photographer of great talent and knowledgeable , enthusiastic of past/present/future Jazz, Rap and Hip Hop, who was able to interview more than sixty of the most noble African American musicians... In her questioning, Desdemona was somehow able to get her subjects to tell some very personal stories."

In our ongoing conversation about this book, Jazz Zoom, Desdemone explains, "You know , I asked everyone for a funny story because I hear Jazz musicians laugh all of the time in back stages. I said, 'What the hell. What are you talking about that makes you laugh and they came up with some very good ones. You know, I thought that would be attractive in a jazz book, especially with interviews.. I first heard some Jazz when I was about twelve years old and I heard some Blues on the radio and I never stopped. It was first Bessie Smith. You know in France, wayback, it was very exceptional to have Jazz on the radio. My friends were all Jazz fans. All of my life I've been listening to Jazz. So when Rap came on , I wasn't surprised. To me, it's one of the stages of African American Music. That's It!!!

Bardin continues, "When I came back here in 1994, I decided to do a book with Jazz Musicians and LeRoy Jenkins said, 'Why don't you make a book about us old Jazz musicians.. I said, ' What a great idea and so I really got all the older ones. It was fun, too. Andrew Cyrille was my son's teacher for four years in the 80's. My son started playing drums when he was three years old. I was in France. Henry Threadgill. David Murray. I have all the best ones"

Desdemone Bardin's photographs of these musicians featured in Jazz Zoom offer us new In _Sight. Shot in Chicago, California and New York with all interviews done face to face, we have something special. She says, "IN person it's always much better because you can have nice vibrations from the person you talk to. David Murray had this big band playing every Monday for a year. So you know I interviewed all of those musicians. I call it Jazz Zoom in the 90's."

Albert Ayler died in 1970. His music has since influenced several generations of musicians.

In the mid-1960's many Jazz musicians, most notably the members of the Association for the Advancement of Creative Musicians (AACM), organized themselves for the purpose of controlling their individual and collective destinies. Roscoe Mitchell, saxophonist and co-founder of the Art Ensemble of Chicago, describes the association's role in this fashion: "The Chicago-based AACM was one of the fundamental groups that pointed the way for musicians to seize control of their own destiny, providing employment for its members, and then expanding its activities to other places. For example, I was involved in starting the Creative Artists Collective in Michigan. And, we're still very active today - the New York chapter sponsors concerts on a regular basis."

In fact, the AACM was founded by Muhal Richard Abrams whose active involvement today continues to reinforce the collective. A brilliant pianist in his own right and a man of singular discretion, Muhal is a preeminent personality of African American music over the last 40 years.

AACM NEW YORK CHAPTER, INC.
P.O. Box 187, Times Square Station, New York, N.Y. 10108

PRSRT STD
U.S. POSTAGE
PAID
NEW YORK, N.Y.
Permit No. 5919

THE AMINA CLAUDINE MYERS QUINTET
FEATURING
Amina Claudine Myers (Piano/Voice/Composer)
Andrew Lamb (Saxophone), Ray Mantilla (Percussion),
Radu Williams (Bass), Thurman Barker (Drums)
(((Plus)))
THE OLIVER LAKE BIG BAND
FEATURING
Oliver Lake (Alto-Saxophone/Conductor)
Marty Ehrlich (1st Alto-Saxophone), Jorge Sylvester (2nd Alto-Saxophone),
Erica Lindsey (1st Tenor-Saxophone), John Stubblefield (2nd Tenor-Saxophone),
Howard Johnson (Baritone-Saxophone), Winston Byrd (1st Trumpet),
Peck Allman (2nd Trumpet), Baikida Carroll (3rd Trumpet),
Duane Eubanks (4th Trumpet), Alfred Patterson (1st Trombone),
Josh Roseman (2nd Trombone), Joe Bowie (3rd Trombone),
Donald Glasco (4th Trombone), Michael Cochran (Piano),
Mark Helias (Bass), Otis Brown (Drums)
• • •
Saturday, September 15, 2001 at 8:00 PM
New York Society for Ethical Culture
2 West 64th Street, NYC
(Located at 64th Street & Central Park West)
General Admission - $15.00, Senior Citizens and Students - $8.00 w/Valid I.D.
For Information Call: 212-594-7149

Desdemone Bardin
355 Clinton Ave., #10C
Brooklyn, NY 11238

State of the Arts

NYSCA

THIS EVENT IS MADE POSSIBLE WITH PUBLIC FUNDS FROM THE NEW YORK STATE COUNCIL ON THE ARTS (A STATE AGENCY), AND GRANTS FROM THE HELEN W. BUCKNER RESIDUARY TRUST, AND THE AARON COPLAND FUND FOR MUSIC.

Lester Bowie, a founding member of the Art Ensemble and leader of Brass Fantasy, is one of the foremost musicians who reaped the benefits of AACM support:

Q. Can you talk a little about the AACM?

A. It officially came into existence when the state (Illinois) incorporation papers were filed, but the band itself was formed in 1961. There were a lot of musicians in Chicago that were trying to get the music across - I think of Eddie Harris, but there were many others. The Art Ensemble was begun at the end of 1965, shortly after I arrived in Chicago: when I got there Roscoe (Mitchell) and Joseph (Jarman) already had their own groups as part of the AACM. I went there for a rehearsal. I played a solo and left, but by the time I got home, my phone was ringing and we started rehearsing the next day. All the musicians we played with were drawn from AACM; the concepts as well. We also played a wide variety of music, not only so-called avant garde. Fontella Bass was doing shows with the AACM Big Band: the whole idea was to be creative, get our own venues and places to play. I'd say we're still doing the same thing now.

Q. Besides Roscoe and Joseph, who else was in the Art Ensemble?

A. Malachi Favors and, then, when we went to Paris in 1969, we picked up Don Moye; we knew Don from before, he was in a group from Detroit in the late sixties.

Q. How long has the group been playing together?

A. We're the second oldest group, personnel-wise, in the business.

Q. Were you yourself from a music family?

A. Yeah, my father played trumpet and taught music in classrooms for 30+ years in St. Louis. His father before him was a trombonist - my father is 90, so you can see that my grandfather reaches back into the 1800's. And his father before him was a top organist in church, so my whole family's been in music: my father's brothers were also musicians, as are my two brothers, as are some of my own children.

Q. You recently gathered together the Hip Hop Feelharmonic, a big band of forty musicians and a group of rappers called Get Open. Is this some kind of fusion?

A. It's about music of inclusion, as opposed to music of exclusion. I'd play something "in" and see what I can do with it, rather than say I don't like it or feel it's not up to the level. A lot of people complain about Rap, saying there's not enough music in it. So I thought, "Let's add some!" We took the music these rappers were using and orchestrated it for a large orchestra; that way, we came up with a new reality. The spirit of the rappers is what I enjoy: they're doing something different and we're trying to do something different too. It was natural that we get together.

Q. How about some of these musicians who are serious about "Europeanizing" the music?

A. Some of them have gotten to the point where what they're playing isn't what we know as Jazz. Jazz is an attitude...a concept, not a type of music that you can associate exclusively with Billie Holiday or Miles Davis. Nor does it have to swing. It's getting to the point where Swing means 4/4 (time) means tempo. Swing is about feeling...about motion, not necessarily about tempo. The thing now is to make people think it swings when it doesn't even have a tempo. The music has grown beyond a lot of things: for example, (Anthony) Braxton has gone beyond; he's taken that concept on off... I mean, we can play anything, absorb any music... there's no limit, no boundaries. Our shit is beyond the people who are trying to define it.

Q. Have you got a funny story to tell?

A. Miles (Davis) was like a stand-up comedian. In his book and in answer to who his favorite trumpet players were, my name was the first to come up, and I felt really honored and surprised. He was such a funny guy, and there is a short story that occurred between him and me. My wife and I as well as Phillip Wilson and his wife were invited to dinner at the home of an Italian friend, right across the street from Miles' house. So after we had finished dinner and drunk a lot of wine, they told me to go knock on Miles' door. Now this was like 1:00 AM in the morning. So we went over and rung the bell. The speaker phone came on: a female voice asked, "Who is it?" I said, "It's Lester Bowie." First...silence, then she asked, "What instrument do you play?" I answered, "Trumpet." More silence, then she asks, "Where you from?" I say, "St. Louis." More silence, then I hear all these doors unlocking, then Miles appears in his robe. He says, "I was fucking..." I said, "Miles, you know you're dick don't get hard no more, you got anything to drink..."

So we went in and Miles was telling stories. He was even telling my wife, Phillip and his wife, "Now, Lester is a great trumpet player, I really like Lester... Come on Lester, play a note for us." He turns to his girl, "Go get my horn, Lester's going to play for us." Now, I'm thinking to myself, "Man, I don't want to play." You just don't pick up a trumpet and play; you gotta warm up... So, I wasn't into playing, but Miles was saying, "Come on Lester, man...he's great! Play something." Finally, I said "O.K., I'll play." So I took his horn and blew a note, trying to warm it up. As soon I blew that note, Miles got the most pained expression you can imagine on his face: "Aw, man, I thought you could play. You ain't shit, Lester!"

Lester Bowie, the Hip Hop Feelharmonic (40 musicians) plus the rap group Get Open.

Leroy Jenkins has composed two operas, "The Mother of My Three Sons" and "Fresh Faust",
one Jazz opera, "The Three Willies", and a cantata, "The Negro Burial Ground".

1969 Paris violon

LEROY JENKINS

I started studying the violin when I was eight years old. My mother bought me a half-size violin, and I soon started playing in the Ebenezer Baptist Church in Chicago.

Q. Were you influenced by church music?

A. Yes, church hymns and Gospel, but also Rhythm & Blues and Big Band Jazz of the 1940's. I was playing one and listening to the others. In the last year of grammar school, I wanted to play in the school marching band, so I started playing the clarinet. My dad went out to buy me a clarinet...off the street. Since he didn't know anything about instruments, some guy sold him an oboe, telling him it was a clarinet. I was really ashamed when the captain of the school band told us to take out our clarinets and I pulled out this oboe. The captain was pleasantly surprised, though, because as band director, he needed oboes so he offered to buy it from my father. So my dad took the money and bought me a silver clarinet, and I started playing in the school marching band. The captain saw I was a good musician and got me to play the bassoon in the school concert band. And, I was playing saxophone in the school Jazz band. I'd only play the violin at teas, luncheons and weddings: those were the kinds of gigs we had..."Drink To Me Only With Thine Eyes" and other tunes by Black classical composers like Cameron White. That's how I got into the music business.

Q. So how did you come to play with Anthony Braxton in Paris?

A. That was years later. I'm another generation than Braxton. I'm a Bebopper! When I was a teenager, I would listen to Charley Parker and Dizzy Gillespie. Bird is my man, that's why I played saxophone - they called me 'Little Bird'. That was a badge of honor. While I continued to play all the other instruments in college at Florida A & M., I majored in violin. After college, I went to Mobile, Alabama for four years to teach violin in the segregated schools of the South. I went back to Chicago after that because I wanted to play, I was tired of teaching, and there I got reacquainted with Muhal (Richard Abrams) who was already an accomplished musician making some money. The AACM was just getting ready to be formed. It must have been in the mid-1960's when I met Anthony Braxton, and we formed this group with Leo Smith and others and started playing around Chicago. But it's not a very good town to ply your musical trade, so Braxton, Leo and I decided in 1969 to go to Paris, and that's when I started living off my music.

Q. How does classical/modern music fit in with jazz?

A. Because the violin is considered a classical music instrument, there were always a lot of opportunities in that direction, so I always straddled the two fields. But my background is Blues, Jazz and Gospel, so that always works itself into any kind of music I might play. Throughout the 1970's here in New York, I was doing a lot of playing, and writing a little, you know, for mixed quintet, trio, Anthony Braxton Quartet, and solo. The last group I had was "Sting", an urban Blues group. That was before the arrival of the eighties and Ronald Reagan; after that, every day of that decade was conservative. Music tastes turned away from avant garde Jazz and all the music innovators were being put down.

Very soon I found myself unable to work, not making a living. It was frightening. Then I discovered that there were several white, middle class musicians and composers who were into the new Classical music and avant garde Jazz; they knew my music and appreciated it. The new music people were checking me out more than the Jazz crowd, so I decided maybe I should start writing compositions for the classical players to teach them how to improvise. I wrote the first piece for the Brooklyn Philharmonic.

Actually, I'm living the life as an artist, I'm doing projects, either performing or writing compositions. It's not like the old days when one was a starving artist. I'm too old to starve, even though I'm often on the brink.

Q. You must have had some unusual things happen to you?

A. In 1978-79, I was invited to Cremona, Italy to perform on a Stradivarius violin which was in the museum there. When I came to town, the guys who picked me up at the train station said, "We haven't gotten the O.K. yet from the city fathers." So I waited in the hotel room, walking around...waiting around, until they got the green light and called to tell me to come downstairs immediately. So I ran downstairs, wearing only my pants and a T-shirt and got in the car. They took me to this museum where everything was decorated in maroon - the couches, the seats, the cushions, and even the tables.

And there was the Stradivarius in a plexiglass display case. This guy pushed a button, the door opened, and they took it out. Ah, the Strad! At that time, it was worth $300,000. Some of the bigwigs of the museum were there, and so I started playing: it was just so exciting to be playing a Stradivarius violin, I just played on but was really careful not to damage it.

"Okay", they said, "we're going to play in the piazza." They put the violin in a case and gave it to me. Two police officers in Italian summer wear - you know, white tunics and blue pants with the red stripe down the side - marched me to the car. I got in the back seat with the violin, they got in the front, and there was another car in back. I said to myself, "If the guys could see me now, the police are taking me to the gig! OooWee!"

When I got to the piazza, they had people lined up waiting for the free concert. It was July and very hot there. I played for about forty-five minutes. Was I sweating! I usually don't sweat like that, but since I was only wearing a wide T-shirt, the instrument was touching my body and the sweat was going all over the instrument.

The custodian of the violin was motioning for me to stop, but I just kept playing. Finally, I played my whole repertoire and it was great. The crowd loved it. The violin was fantastic! I mean, I could do anything. I didn't want to give it back.

But after I was through, they repossessed the violin from me. I was angry...very angry, you know, that they wouldn't let me keep it! When the violin left, the police left too. It was like I was Cinderella - without that instrument, I went back to rags again.

The Negro Burial Ground: a Cantata for the Departed.
Tells of the discovery of a cemetery in Lower Manhattan where perhaps 20,000 slaves were buried.

Composition 102: Ghost Trance music for large ensemble with three giant puppets

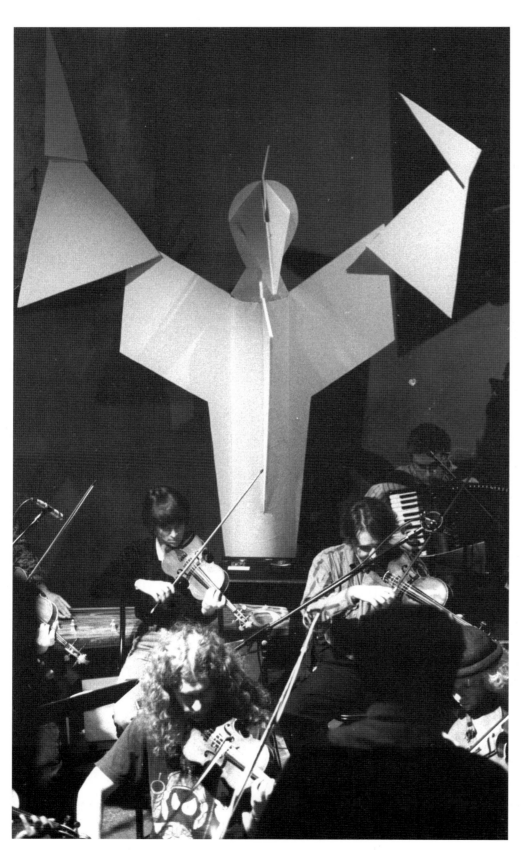

Q. Would you please briefly describe your involvement with AACM?

A. Back in Chicago, I was very affected and inspired by Joseph Jarman who had a very interesting dramatic component in his work. He brought something very fresh to imagery and the restructure of music during that period.

Q. When did you conceive and start combining your music with the dynamics of visual art?

A. My decision to move toward composite aesthetic approaches came about as a result of my need to reestablish the relationship with song form. By 1980 I realized that I didn't have very much vocal music, despite my great interest in it, so I sought a way to reconnect with it. I was looking for something more than structural intellectualism as a basis for evolving my music, and found that narrative structures would give me the possibility of building Tri-Metric models that could reflect individual experience and symbolic experience.

So I went back and started to study the trans-European opera tradition, the American song form tradition. I've always been a great fan of Johnny Mathis, Frank Sinatra, Sammy Davis, Jr. and, more and more, I would find that storytelling would give me the possibility to move closer to dream postulation, the possibility of finding a surprise as a means of reflecting my experience and disenchantment with the idea of just total freedom or total structuralism. I'm equally not interested in either one, but rather looking for a balance. So my compositions sought to create a positive fantasy state, conducive to the children and consistent with my love of puppetry. My "composition 102" is dedicated to that American puppeteer master, Jim Henson: it gave me the opportunity to create a fantasy context and, inside of that context, detail the movements of three giant puppets which intersect with the internal logic of the music.

So, by 1980 I had determined that the medium of opera, (incorporating story and dialogue) would be very important to me because of its narrative structures. I wanted a music that would

have mutable, stable syntheses. The "Trillium" operas are connected to the "Tri-Axium" writings, that is, they are the second partial of the "Tri-Axium" writings. "Trillium" is a state of dialogues that permitted me to extend language and music devices of my system into the symbolic. Inside of "Trillium" is a set of movement, that is, there is an improvisational logic, there's notated logic, the correspondence logic that involves body movements and switching. "Trillium" is past, present and future at once.

Q. Can you describe how you mix musical genr to come up with this "new" music?

A. The music that my Tri-Centric Orchestra is playing in this period is called the "Ghost Trance" Music. These musics are a prototype that was conceived to be a trans-music in the great tradition of the "Trance Persian" musics, music of the "American Indian Trance", musics as they relate to transcendent states; and so the "Ghost Trance" musics are an attempt to establish a music state that will allow for ver long compositions to take place, compositions that also have metric rhythm, compositions that will give a new sense of spatial definition and time-lift strategies. This is a post-nuclear structure.

Anthony Braxton in concert (Paris 1969) playing percussion instruments, including an eggbeater.

WARREN SMITH drummer

Q. Can you think of an exceptional circumstance that occurred during your career?

A. You know, I remember a performance we did in my studio one night several years ago. The clock had just stroked 12, and we decided to play Thelonius Monk's 'Round Midnight'. When we started out, and I had perhaps forgotten about the neighbors who might have been trying to sleep, I gave the drums a thunderclap-type roll - Boom! - and the band joined in. The first time I looked up, there were two policemen standing in front of me: the older of the two cops raised his hands like a conductor and shouted, 'Hands off!' There was absolute silence in the house. The cop says, 'You gotta be kidding!' Everybody started laughing and that got the cops laughing too.

Q. Last night I heard you play with Anthony Braxton, but I don't know whether what I heard can be called Jazz?

A. I think we're all victimized by labels. For example, there was tremendous resistance from the Swing era to Bebop and from Bebop to Free Jazz. And I myself can be just as guilty of such limited vision: I remember criticizing Coltrane for experimenting on stage...because, for me at that time, performance was something that you rehearsed and rehearsed until perfection, so that you just weren't supposed to do otherwise. So I think the more people hear this music, even though they'll categorize it, I think they won't tend to separate it from the Jazz tradition. I mean, I compose music that is dissonant and that doesn't always have a steady pulse, and I found a way to like it because of consistent exposure. And while I still listen a lot to Art Blakey and Max Roach, I also want to extend the music beyond its traditional sounds and form.

Q. How do you see the future of this music?

A. The good thing is that people are reaching back and playing music which originated late in the last century, and listeners appreciate that as much as what is to come. What you're hearing now is not the final step: technology and people's ability will stretch these concepts to newer dimensions which have yet to be discovered, even though the media may choose to ignore it or even attempt to suppress it.

See, another error we make in this country is to associate a musician with just one type of music, when there are many players who are able to go back and forth between styles with equal proficiency. So if, by stretching out in new directions, we are somehow 'unfaithful' to the tradition, that really is just another way of denying the breadth of our talent and abilities. I mean, those are the same accusations that were leveled at Miles when he ventured into Rock & Roll...

I don't think this music will ever be the most popular in the world. Remember, listeners have to learn to appreciate many of the music's intricacies and, almost, get involved - at least, as real fans! So, it probably won't even attain the popularity that Louis Armstrong enjoyed in his heyday. But it will retain an audience comparable to that of symphonic music. We have to overcome obstacles which a listener may bring along so that there can be a back and forth.

On percussion with Anthony Braxton's large ensemble.

Q. Are there links between your music and the poetry of Derek Wolcott?

A. All kinds of art - painting, literature, etc. - have things in common, it's just the manifestation that is different. So once an artist discovers that, it's easy to turn to other mediums, whether it be dance, poetry or architecture, anything that will stimulate you, sometimes even more than the medium you usually work in.

Q. I find the way you created a structure around the spoken word to be beautiful!

A. The structure of the poetry determines the structure of the music. The poetry has a rhythm and meter, it has time built into it - if you don't observe the time, you won't understand the text. So, once you understand the poetry, you know what to do with it musically. My structure is always the result of a process, it does not come in the beginning to me. Once something comes into existence, it will have form. If it's correct and strong, it doesn't have to fit any other ideas of structure: it'll still be 100% correct.

Q. Does the poet's style influence your music?

A. No, but it influences my perspective - how to do it!

Q. It sounds pretty surrealistic at times?

A. Yes.

Q. Has the fact that you've lived in India changed your musical style?

A. I think that whenever you've expanded your life from one part of the world to another and gather in new information and perspective, you don't even have to think about it, it just happens.
Once you change location from one part of the world to another and actually mingle with people there and their rhythm of life and the smell of life...and death, it transforms you.

Q. A well-known band of yours is called "Very Very Circus". Why did you choose that name?

A. It's about rings. A big circus has more than one ring operating - things are going on here and over here too. So there are things going on simultaneously and on the same level.

Music/Theater

On Walcott
Threadgill's new music performed by a small orchestra with the text of *Derek Walcott* read by *Avery Brooks*, choreography by *Judith Sanchez* and visuals by *Jules Alan*.

Conduction℠ No. 119
Morris' latest Conduction explores "a view from where you have been to where you are going" using an ensemble of musicians from the Harlem community.
Fri., Oct. 26 & Sat., Oct. 27 @ 8pm-$25, $20

Window on New Work with Morris
Observe an open rehearsal with a discussion on his orchestration method of Conduction.
Thurs., Oct. 18 @ 7pm-$10
(Free for 10/26 or 10/27 ticket holders)

Call **212-650-7100** for information & for tickets call *ticketmaster* at **212-307-7171** or visit www.ticketmaster.com

ADH's Music Series is sponsored by **ABSOLUT VODKA**

Aaron Davis Hall
Harlem's Principal Center for the Performing Arts
W. 135 St. & Convent Ave.,
New York, NY 10031

Desdemone Bardin
355 Clinton Ave., #10C
Brooklyn, NY 11238

(left to right) - Jose Davila, Ted Daniel, Henry Threadgill, Leroy Jenkins.

Music by Anthony Davis, Libretto by Thulani Davis, Story by Christopher Davis.

Q. Do you feel that your music has moved away from the traditional Jazz structures?

A I compose opera and works for orchestra, but I know that my music is a logical extension of Monk, Mingus and Ellington. I feel tied to that tradition but not limited by it, in the sense of having to write music in 4/4 time that swings. Rather, it frees me to follow my own direction which is not necessarily the esthetic defined by the past. Everyone has a different relationship to the tradition, some use it to set up boundaries, others use it as the basis for a new relationship. Jazz is the most important musical tradition in America and critical to defining what serious American music is. And, moreover, as a performer that's what I play - I'm an improviser, that's where my strength is; I don't really enjoy sitting down and playing notated music.

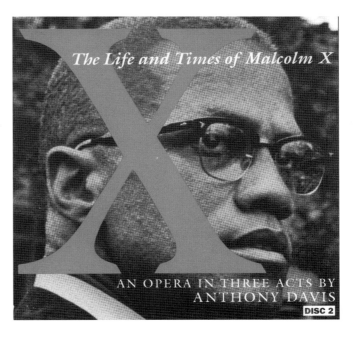

The Life and Times of Malcolm X

AN OPERA IN THREE ACTS BY ANTHONY DAVIS

DISC 2

Q. Do you have a funny story or anecdote to tell?

A. I was in Liverpool for the premiere of "X, The Life and Times of Malcolm X", and doing an interview for a radio show with the BBC. From the hotel lobby, this guy with a very British-accent called me on the house phone and asked, "What is this interesting opera you've written, 'Malcolm the 10th?" I was able to stop laughing long enough to tell him, "X, man! X!"

Fontella Bass and the Lafayette Inspirational Ensemble

Q. I understand you came up singing Gospel?

A. Well, I was brought up in the church as a child. As a matter of fact, I was playing in mortuaries at the age of five. We had two prominent Black funeral homes in the neighborhood and I played for both of them, my grandmother and I. We were playing songs like "What a Friend We Have in Jesus" and "Near the Cross". That's really why I don't go to funerals today or bake any more cakes: as a kid, I used to bake cakes on the summer weekends to raise funds so I could go to the National Baptist Convention in August every year.

Q. Who have you been playing with through the years?

A. Well, back in 1970-71, I sang for the soundtrack of the film, "Les Stances à Sophie", a film by French director Agnes Varda for which the Art Ensemble of Chicago did the soundtrack. I also did three or four albums with them. At the time, Lester (Bowie) and I owned a home together outside of Paris and had set up a camping site away from the house, where the AACM musicians would stay. I remember Leroy (Jenkins), with whom I'd practice on piano, came out back one morning and woke us up, practicing his violin scales! What a delightful awakening.

Then when I came home, I got with a label called Parlor Records out of Shreveport, Louisiana. I had several little minor "hits" out of there. Then I got with Epic Records in 1978 and recorded two or three numbers, but lost out when the administration changed. When I got to Nonesuch Records, I rerecorded the songs I'd done on a solo album called "Everlasting Love" with a full band. In between time, I recorded the album "Breath of Life" with the World Saxophone Quartet and still often play with them as well as my own instrumental group.

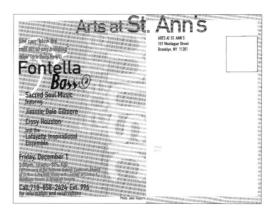

Q. I heard this beautiful piece entitled "Jupiter" that you composed: are many musicians of your generation composers as well?

A. Many are. When I was coming up, my first idol was Clifford Brown; I also liked Art Blakey and followed those who were playing that style of music. To learn to play like that, you have to study so many scales and chords and rudiments and theory, and you find out that it's more interesting than just trying to play. As a trumpet player, I can only play one note at a time, but my curiosity led me to discover how you move from one cluster of notes to another and another, all the while maintaining continuity.

Q. Are you continuing in the astral vein?

A. "Jupiter" was written in 1970, though it's a recent arrangement, and back then I was running on high energy. I'm kind of surprised that the one I'm working on now also features high energy and a relaxed, trance-like quality. What I would like to do now is travel in outer space: I wrote one like that called "Cosmic Dreams". From what I've seen of that vastness out there, no matter how fast you go, it always seems like you're going slow. I'm fascinated with the idea of time - in other words, two or three objects on the same trajectory but traveling at different speeds, and that's how I try to write my music.

Several years ago, I had discussions with musicians who were consciously trying not to swing, but I myself don't function very well in total freedom, though I have played in those situations. You might say that my collaboration with other musicians is a continuous conversation - I feed off them and expect them to do the same off me. When I write, there must be structure - rhythmic, harmonic, whatever...

I really need the use of a symphony orchestra because that's got the instrumentation and the colors to bring out the best in my music.

THE MUHAL RICHARD ABRAMS' EXPERIMENTAL BAND

FEATURING:

LEROY JENKINS (VIOLIN)
WADADA LEO SMITH (TRUMPET)
FRANK GORDON (TRUMPET)
GEORGE LEWIS (TROMBONE)
ROSCOE MITCHELL (REEDS)
JOSEPH JARMAN (REEDS)
HENRY THREADGILL (REEDS)
WALLACE MCMILLAN (REEDS)
AMINA CLAUDINE MYERS (PIANO)
LEONARD JONES (BASS)
THURMAN BARKER (PERCUSSION)
REGGIE NICHOLSON (DRUMS)
AND
MUHAL RICHARD ABRAMS (PIANO)

BEFORE WE BEGIN WE ASK THAT THERE BE NO AUDIO OR VIDEO TAPE RECORDING, NO PHOTOGRAPHING, AND NO SMOKING. SINCE SOME PEOPLE IN THE PAST HAVE ELECTED TO DISREGARD THE PROHIBITION ON PHOTOGRAPHING, AUDIO AND VIDEO TAPE RECORDING, WE MUST WARN YOU THAT ANYONE FOUND VIOLATING THESE RULES WILL BE ASKED TO LEAVE PROMPTLY.

WE THANK YOU FOR YOUR COOPERATION.

I remember hearing Dizzy say, "Music is still a business!" It's not only important that you play the instrument well, but you've also got to market yourself. Or sometimes, when the media is looking for something different and you just happen to have it, then attention will come to you. Louis Armstrong and Dizzy Gillespie were into entertaining the audience; I've also heard of saxophonists who would play standing up on the bar and the audience loved it. And then in the fifties, Miles comes along and...

Q. Turns his back to the audience.

A. That was in the sixties. In the fifties, Miles stopped talking to the audience. For so many years, Jazz musicians would talk to the spectators, and here comes this one guy who does something different. I know Dizzy said perhaps Miles thought it was enough to come and entertain, and that he didn't feel the need to talk. I also know that Miles said that he would turn his back to different spots of the stage because it gave him a better sound .

Q. In his autobiography, he said he turned his back to the audience so that he could see the other musicians... I think Miles also questioned why a musician needed to be a clown on stage... Times were changing!

A. Yeah, but what he did at the time he decided to do it was perfect timing, because a lot of people were looking for a change. If you look at Louis Armstrong as a former star of the music scene, and then at Dizzy Gillespie and Charlie Parker who were leaders of their particular era, what Miles did was a real break with tradition...

Q. Okay, but there's a lot of humor in what Dizzy would say to the audience, though I know that Louis smiling all the time was disapproved of...

A. When Louis was doing it, not that many years separated him from slavery, so he still felt he had to be subservient, very polite, a Step'n'Fetchit kind of persona. Whereas Dizzy came to prominence when there was still a lot of racial tension in the U.S., but not as much as before, so he was able to add some comical humor as a natural part of his performance.

When I was younger, I would hear musicians, my peers, saying they would never do what Louis and Dizzy did, but my older brother and my teachers had already thought about it: they said, 'If we had been in that position back then, we would have had no choice! If you want to make a living in a certain time period, you have to go along with what's goin' on.' Miles, on the other hand, did his thing after Rosa Parks refused to move to the back of the bus, Martin Luther King, Jr. was leading marches all over the South; it was timely. Can you imagine if Miles had come along in Louis' or Dizzy's time and turned his back on a southern audience during a concert? He would not have survived!

AARON STEWART tenor saxophone player
ALEX HARDING baritone saxophone player

(left to right) Alex Harding, Aaron Stewart, at Society for Ethical Culture.

Chuck Stewart's classic photo of John Coltrane via the Schomberg Center for Research of Black Culture, New York City

Alex Harding

If you go back to the sixties and Coltrane and Joe Henderson, the evolution of Jazz was a conciousness movement - understanding oneself, Black militancy, Malcolm X, Martin Luther King: it was a time to be proud of who you were, and the music spoke of that.

Aaron Stewart

Q. Having played with Muhal Richard Abrams and Andrew Hill, and knowing your admiration for the World Saxophone Quartet musicians, how do you expect to extend the music?

A. There are, I believe, many different possibilities for the music's future development. Perhaps the most fundamental of these is an inquiry into the laws of rhythm as they manifest themselves in music. When I talk about "rhythm", I mean the structure and placement of events in musical space and time, whether the music concerned is "free" or "in time". As for the "free" musics, there has been a great deal of research in this area by the various members of AACM, who have also been in the vanguard of new developments in the field of notated music that is played "in time".

I don't view the issue of playing "in time", or "out of time" from a dualistic, either/or perspective. I was exposed to the continuum of the music as a whole, as opposed to learning about only one period or group of artists, like the musicians who developed "Bebop". As a result, I see the myriad types of "free" playing as being tributaries of the larger creative enterprise that the music as a whole represents. There is nothing antithetical about the relationship between the musics of, say, Cecil Taylor and Bud Powell, or Muhal Richard Abrams and Duke Ellington.

There are also many areas that have not yet been explored in the field of music that involves the use of a fixed pulse. The preeminent exponent of this line of inquiry during this time period is probably Steve Coleman, one of the most important musical thinkers to emerge in the last 20 years. As a devotee of Coleman's music, as well as the traditional musics of the non- western world in Africa, India, Korea, etc., it is very clear to me that there are rhythmic techniques in existence that "jazz", for all its creative brilliance, has yet to touch on.

JOHN COLTRANE

Q. Are you projecting a new outlook for the 21st century?

A. I am developing a new sound: it's called the saxello, utilizing electronics and acoustics.

Q. Tell me about yourself?

A. My background is very diverse: I've worked at the top of the Classical, avant garde, Pop and Jazz world. I'm trying to blend that now and become a Classical Jazz player. I'd like to develop Jazz classics through my saxello and bring a new classic sound to the world. This instrument is from so long ago, and so many players like Rahsaan Roland Kirk, Pharaoh Sanders and others played it for a while, then pushed it aside because it had horrific tuning problems. I've spent the last five years plus twenty years on top of that researching the acoustics of the saxophone, including mouthpieces and reeds, and how it matches to the anatomical relationship. I've committed the last five years to the saxello, redesigned the whole basic structure of the instrument with regard to offsetting the notes so that they do play in tune. This new sound has been very well received by the musicians of the World Saxophone Quartet and Reggie Workman, and it's going to be moving ahead to other groups.

I may be the only saxello solo player in the world: others own it and play it as part of their sounds, but they're not soloists...yet! The saxello can cry, it can also laugh: it has all the sounds that many other people reach for another instrument to do. Instead of switching from soprano to alto and so forth, I'll stay with one instrument and make it do what I want. So I think I'm heading for the 21st century.

(left to right) - Marty Ehrlich, John Purcell.

OLIVER LAKE *alto saxophone player*

Q. Did the Free Jazz of the sixties influence you in any way?

A. My introduction to what was called Free Jazz came from the AACM in Chicago, but I must also say that we in St. Louis were doing something similar around that same time. What mainly inspired and excited me about AACM was that they were organized: we would get together, improvise, and then go home; but in Chicago, the musicians would give concerts and be presenting themselves as an organization. After I went to meet Lester (Bowie), Muhal (Richard Abrams) and many others in Chicago, I got back to St. Louis and advised that we should organize ourselves as a branch of the AACM. Instead, in 1967, we organized under the name "Black Artists Group", which included musicians, dancers and actresses, and had exchanges with the AACM between the two cities - we'd rent a bus and take our band to Chicago for a concert, and vice versa.

Q. Do you think that the music called Jazz has consciously reflected the social and political problems of successive epochs, say from the 1920's to the present?

A. Whether or not a Jazz musician is politicized, his music will usually have a social and/or political meaning for the times in which he lives. For myself and from my own observation, I don't think it's a conscious decision to compose or play music which is socially significant; it just kinda happens and there are certain reasons why that happens. I remember when I moved to Paris, in 1974, I met a French guitarist who, after hearing for the first time what we five musicians of the Black Artists Group were playing, asked, "Why are you playing like that? I don't understand!" But after making a trip to New York, he came back and told me, "Now, I understand why you play as you do." That was just his way of saying that our playing was a reflection of life in New York.

Q. Is there a particular format that you prefer to perform in?

A. Well, I've actually played in many different musical settings - with the World Saxophone Quartet, in solo concerts, with my Rhythm & Blues band; I've also composed and played in the traditional big band setting - five saxophones, 4 trumpets and 4 trombones à la Duke Ellington. Now, I'm currently playing in a trio, "Trio Three" (with Reggie Workman and Andrew Cyrille), and I also have a quintet with Jay Hoggard, Charles Eubanks, Cecil Brooks III, and Russell Grad). Once upon a time, Leroy Jenkins and I were doing duo concerts, and I also play in duos with Donal Fox. I 've written orchestral pieces as well as music for chamber groups, such as saxophone and strings, or saxophone and percussion ensembles. They're all one thing to me.

Q. Do you have a story to tell?

A. There's one that I do in my one-man theater piece - you know, it was a series of sketches based upon my observations about the music - Jazz and Rap, for example, which is so popular today - as well as things about my life. Anyway, this group that I had several years ago, called "Jump Up" was invited to Africa. We were in Malawi and all sitting in a restaurant, saying how great it was to be here in Africa, and how this African looked like a relative or friend back in America. So one of us said, "Why don't we ask the waiter what tribe he thinks our guitar player comes from?" Everyone agreed, so we called the waiter over and asked him the question: he fixated his gaze on the guitarist for a short moment and said, "American nigger!"

Q. Would you say that you are the rhythm section of the World Saxophone Quartet, like the brass musicians in James Brown's band of the sixties?

A. Your question really presents your own way of looking at things. I'm not saying that it's true or it's not true. What you will get out of my answer is true, but how it got to that is not true. You see, everybody's trying to make music go in the direction they think it's going in, such as using James Brown's influence on this and that. For example, James' new style of music came about only after the Fender bass was electrified in the fifties: the guitar was already electrified since it was a heavy American instrument coming out of the Blues. But when the bass was electrified, the whole sound changed. James Brown and some more people...Otis Redding, Ike & Tina Turner, etc.

I remember the first time I heard James Brown...in '63. To me, he sounded like Albert Ayler, not the James Brown he evolved into later. It was like he was into some sort of ritual, that man was something else. Highest energy! It was somewhere in Virginia,

I was stationed in Norfolk, and we went to the concert in carloads. There was this real high, 10-12 foot stage and did he rock the place, like in the holiest of churches. Personally, I dug that more than what James got to be later, which was colossal!. But when you live through the era of a guy like that, or part of the era of Duke Ellington, or Joe Louis, or Michael Jordan, or Miles... That's why I see it the way I see it. But I'm an artist; an entertainer's got a whole different program.

Q. How do you see the music scene today?

A. I got to New York City in late 1969 and helped reconstruct the whole music situation here. There was nothing going on at that time and so we launched a counterattack, playing a new kind of music that helped bring us back to where we are now. We had the people, they had the industry. The people said, 'This is what we want!' But one of the things that's wrong is that the industry is promoting musicians who don't know how to play for people. They don't play notes that you can feel. Most of that stuff is too depressing, it makes you feel inadequate if you go for it, you

know...like, you're not something that you should be. It doesn't deal with people, children, life, death, compassion and all those things.

When we play, I don't necessarily need the experience of having played with James Brown 'cause the music I play is OF the people. They're tryin' to act like there's no street music: Bullshit! Street music IS the people's music: the music is always of the people; the people are the music. I'm glad you heard James Brown, but this is not where I'm coming from. I know secular, sacred, academic music and I know the Blues, which is a whole 'nother kind of experience comin' from where we play and they're trying to obliterate it.

(left to right) - Bluiett Baritone Saxophone Group: Bluiett, Patience Higgins, Pablo Calaguer (not pictured) Alex Harding, James Carter, Ronnie Burrage.

was born in 1940 so all that music is basically in my being and way of playing...Jazz, avant garde, whatever. Like they called people Beboppers so they can have these labels, or other kinds of labels, but that's okay with me. Yeah, roots are okay 'cause we bring actuality to the past, not vice versa... People talk about imitating James Brown, Miles, and others. We don't have to do that, but I can conjure that image and those kinds of feelings 'cause the most important part of the music is about Black people in America. Whatever the end result is, they can't leave that out, it's impossible.

So, the cats whom I've basically been associated with for these last thirty-three years have really advanced music beyond the catchism they're trying to sell. Anyway, we've got to deal with it now 'cause this shit's in deep, deep bad trouble. They're talking about elevating the level of concerts, but they haven't got anybody like Michael Jordan to slam dunk and just make people excited enough to come see it. That's because of the control factor: music...that can't be seen nor touched, but you've got to control it. So, at least, the people I play with have got that much sense, and I'm glad of that.

When the industry came along and tried to bump us off with this newer crop, I just said "later", took hold of this new, old horn and went back to doing what I knew from the beginning, what I really feel and think, not what the so-called "knowledgeable" folk say.

RONNIE BURRAGE drummer

Q. What do you think of these "Banlieues Bleues" concerts (1), especially since you played with the World Saxophone Quartet?

A. For me, the workshops everyday with the French kids stood out. The music wasn't complex, and I'm sure David (Murray) composed it with that in mind, but it was good to see it take shape. I mean, a lot of these people have only been playing a few months and, still, they all wanted to learn. I love to teach anyway: I spent 5 years teaching drums and a Jazz ensemble at the University of the Arts in Philadelphia; I've also taught in the PHD program at the University of Berlin.

Q. Has music always been a part of your life?

A. I started playing with McCoy Tyner at the age of seventeen-eighteen, and I'm going on thirty-nine now. I'm not about getting paid or having recognition. It may bother me sometimes because I go places and people don't know who I am. But I have several ensembles under my own name and have done hundreds of CD's - all different: most recently, I played drums for Hamiet Bluiett's Baritone Saxophone Group and produced the CD on the Knitting Factory label.

(1) Annual Jazz festival which takes place every March/April in the northern outskirts of Paris.

Q. Would you say that New York is still the Jazz 'Mecca'?

A. You know, I come from Detroit where people enjoy playing many different kinds of music, the radio was always working. I recently saw this article about the sad state of New York radio: well New York radio has been sad for a long period of time compared to Detroit.

For working musicians, the biggest turnaround came as I pretty much watched the natural ebb and flow of work, the rise and fall of values in New York - and we're seeing a consistent downward spiral; this used to be a place where art was the driving force, but now it's more like real estate. You know, people talk about NYC as the greatest city in the world...for what? For...

Q. Money!

A. Yeah! But, at least we still have live music going on, we're not dead like L.A. in that regard. I've done some things, other than music, in interactive expressions - for example, I worked with writers like Ntozake Shange, Jessica Hagedorn, Thulani Davis... I must owe that to my father who had me reading poetry early on, and I took a liking to Paul Lawrence Dunbar, probably the first African American, artistic, linguistic specialist. I'm also able to enjoy the work of painters - artists in residence like Ed Clark, Michael Kelly Williams - whom I met during the Studio Museum of Harlem's activities. I mean, I'm most excited about any collaborative effort - it doesn't even have to be artists. Maybe a project has too many artists, maybe the necessary interactive action should be coming from different disciplines or walks of life, so that we'd all be looking for common ground. It might also facilitate the realization that what passes for culture in this 2-3-400 year- old U.S. madness is a puddle compared to the ocean of a society with more than 2,000 years of existence.

Q. What do you think about this new African American music?

A. Listeners who come expecting to hear one kind of music and are disappointed because another kind of music is played are really the ones at fault. The audience has got to realize that something CAN happen, but it won't always happen when they want it to happen. Music can sometimes drive you out the door, like when the yogis give a boost to your kundalini - some people are happy, other are crying, some can't take it...

Well, it's the same with this music. The experience that you have at the time - your reaction to it - is not exactly what is going on. There's gonna be stuff that you won't understand or like; you won't even know why you had to experience it until maybe 20 years later, and then...'Oh, THAT'S why!' It's like my juvenile aversion to Mozart: my brother and I would play a game called "Who's the Composer", and every time I'd hear music I didn't like, I'd guess, 'Mozart!'

DONAL FOX piano player
CAROL AMBER gospel vocalist and piano player

DONAL FOX

Q. Does SWING define Jazz music?

A. I think Swing has to be defined more broadly than that, it's not just (counts out aloud) 'chu ch-ch chu ch-ch chu', which is a rhythmical impulse. The Marsalis plan defines Jazz in terms of one type of Swing - strong beat moving forward like a locomotive. But Duke Ellington wrote Swing tunes that were looping and light. Or a ballad where the emphasis is not on tapping the toe but on the lyrical, the melodic and the emotional. By overly emphasizing Swing, you can narrow the music.

Q. Aren't the most popular musics among the masses those that have a regular rhythm?

A. I call it harmonic motion, but there's also a rhythm in our speech - a sense of energy and forward motion.

Q. And syncopation...

A. And the bass lines. The way the harmony works - the 'chacone', you know, repeats the chord with changes in the baroque which are cyclical, and very similar to the song form in Jazz. I mean, look...with just a baseline and drums, how the Swingle Singers sang.

Q. Will the new music of the 21st century fuse the African American and modern Classical?

A. If you're a musician, you're open to sound. You might like sound "y"
over there and sound "x" over here, and then somebody tells you
that "x" is labeled   so-and-so; it doesn't matter if
that sound inspires you and can be incorporated
into your music. The people who are trying
to separate you from that sound are
ignorant of the history of their
own music. If they codify
it so that outside
influences
are shut out, the music will surely shut down.   Nevertheless, World Music will also have
the effect of opening things up.   I've got a strong Classical background, as did
S c o t t   J o p l i n ,   A r t   T a t u m   a n d   B u d   P o w e l l .

What I do in my own writing now is, for example, when I write a concert piece, it's notated and
improvised, but notated in a way so that you can't tell when the improvisation
begins or ends; they blend together. And you should hear some of
these classically-trained musicians, once they get over
their formal training of playing only what is
is notated on the score and start to
get comfortable with
improvised
music.

CAROL AMBER

Q. Do you only sing Gospel music?

A. Yes, now I do. I've explored many other kinds but have come back to Gospel where I belong. My mother and father both sang in the chorus of the Metropolitan Opera when she was pregnant with me so when she went to rehearsal, I was there. And after she had me, I'd have to sit out in the audience when they had rehearsal, and she told me I never made a peep...as if I was soaking everything up. So I've got opera in me- my mother is a lyric soprano and my father is a baritone bass. And the church I grew up in, it was Lutheran, the music is straight up and down there. And then I went over the AME church where there was Classical music and Gospel music, and it was all good.

Q. How does Gospel fit in with Jazz music?

A. It fuses with it naturally. Bluiett, for example, knows how to use my inspirational songs in his Jazz repertoire, though this might take the audience by surprise. But then again, Gospel music these days has really taken a turn: you've got the hard core, (counts off briskly by clapping) 1-2-3-4, 1-2-3-4, and the contemporary Gospel, Gospel Jazz and, lately, Gospel Rap. It has really broadened up.

Q. Well, Jazz and Gospel don't have the same rhythm but they have the beat in common. Is that why they fuse naturally?

A. You know, I had to ask a musician that question. He said, 'That's a very good question.' He thought about it a while and gave me an answer that I've taken and accepted ever since. He said, 'Jazz is on the 2 and the 4, Gospel is on the 1 and the 3.' (Sings "Sunny Side of the Street" and claps on the 2nd and 4th strong beats. Then sings two bars of "I Love to Praise Him" and taps the rhythm out accenting the 1st and 3rd beats). But it's the same beat!

Q. What do you think of the evolution of Jazz and the musics that fuse with it in the nineties?

A. Well, you know, I think Jazz's essence allows it to welcome music and influences from other cultures, like John Coltrane's exploration of East Indian music and Don Cherry playing with Gamelleon. The only thing that limits Jazz is the media, critics, retailers and record company moguls simply because they want something they can identify. Oliver Lake has this great poem about bringing my food on the same plate - 'first, the salad, then the meat: Marvin Gaye, Dizzy Gillespie, Aretha Franklin, all the same, all one.'

Q. Can fusing with another style be a way of engendering a different kind of creativity?

A. For some of us it's a natural connection as opposed to a conscious decision to...say mix Funk with... You know, it's not a decision since this is how I hear it: I write the drum and bass parts and it sounds like some Funk/HipHop stuff, and I write the horn line and it sounds like some cutting-edge Jazz; and they go together. If you're true to your influences, you end up mixing these things together. Doesn't that reflect our day and age as well as this country's diversity?

Q. Do you have a funny story to tell?

A. I have a 14-piece band called New Yoruba, which is a synthesis of African folklore, mostly from Cuba, and contemporary Jazz; we performed for the first time in 1983 at the Public Theater - the band included Bob Stewart, Howard Johnson, Rasul Siddik, Oliver Lake, Baikida Carroll, John Stubblefield, Rufus Reid, Kelvin Bell, Pheeroan akLaff, and some incredible percussionists, including Orlando Puntilla and Eddie Rodriguez. It was in 1984 when New Yoruba first toured Europe. We had a bus to get us around, but the driver seemed to think we were his worst nightmare: he'd get bugged when someone needed to go to the bathroom; or, every musician had a tape of his own music, and we'd play it loud, day or night, driving to or from tour stops. It had to be very late one night, and everyone was asleep; there was not a sound, no music was playing. The driver decided to play something that he liked, though I don't remember what it was. Not a minute had passed before John Stubblefield's voice boomed from the back of bus, 'Turn that shit off!'°

Q. I understand that you're doing a book?

A. Yes, on the music of the GNAWA people of Morocco whom I've known since 1967. These are great musicians and very spiritual people who live in Casablanca, Rabat and elsewhere.

Q. Are your own concerts confined to the U.S.?

A. No, I travel to Europe, Africa and the Caribbean, in addition to gigs in this town and cities like Chicago and San Francisco.

Q. But your "home " base is here?

A. My bases are in Marrakech and Brooklyn, and you might add Paris to them too; I've got three.

Q. Do you usually work with different musicians?

A. Not really! I like to play with musicians who know my music. Sometimes I do solo piano, and other times it could depend if I'm playing with a big band as opposed to a small group. The constant is that I play African music wherever I go and whomever I play with - we play it here, but African music is also played in Brazil, in Cuba, in Jamaica. We are African Americans, but the way we approach music is just like our ancestors did a thousand years ago. That's why we go to Africa, to study the tradition and understand that we do things the same way as our ancestors - the same approach to life, the same approach to music. So, I don't call my music Jazz, I call it "African Rhythms." Although I'm considered a Jazz musician, we ourselves don't even know what the hell the word "Jazz" means. Nobody knows. But when I say African Rhythms, that way we can trace it back to a continent, to a very strong culture. We've managed to survive despite slavery and all the other horrible things that happened to our people. And wherever you find African people, we produce beautiful things.

Just let me say that I'm happy there is recognition today of African music and culture. When I was a kid, there was no such thing as African civilization. The biggest joy for me now is to hear young musicians talking about Africa. Maybe the funniest anecdote of all would be the fact that this GNAWA record, which is all traditional music except for one song that I play, has been nominated for a Grammy. That blows my mind because it's not Afro-Pop, it's traditional, spiritual music, about creation, about God. Many listeners don't know about the spiritual music of Africa which is the beginning of the spiritual music we play here, like the Gospel.

Herman Sonny Blount, better known as Sun Ra, died in 1994, leaving behind a prodigious body of musical works, infused with cosmic mysticism and an infinite number of styles. A talented pianist in his own right, Sun Ra founded and directed one of Jazz's last great big bands from the 1950's until his death: the Arkestra has devoted itself to playing its creator's music, during his life and after.

Among the many musicians who played with Sun Ra, Marshall Allen, Vincent Chancey, Dick Griffin Craig Harris, Jaribu Shahid and Ahmed Abdullah have vivid impressions of him.

Sun Ra and June Tyson.

Q. How would you characterize Sun Ra's legacy to the evolution of Jazz from the 1950's to the nineties?

A. Sun Ra had these new sounds in him when he came onto the scene and would adapt them to the musicians who came to play with him. He was always saying that these new sounds were for tomorrow: the audience might not have understood them then, but they would today!

Q. When did you first play with him?

A. I joined up in 1958 in Chicago. A radio DJ gave me a demo tape with Sun Ra's music on it. Then, a trumpet player I knew told me Sun Ra was playing over at the Ballroom on the South Side and that "he was always looking for new talent." So I went over there, stayed for the gig, and then stayed up all night with him - all he did was talk! And every day I'd come, he'd just talk! One day, he invited me over to John Gilmour's house to hear what I could do. When I got there, John was asleep but there was Sun Ra at the piano so I started playing and here we are.

Q. Did he talk to you about his cosmic ideas?

A. Yeah, all the time, but back then nobody was talking about things like that, so it was all new to me! He'd say, "Believe it or not!", and the only thing I knew for sure was that he was playing good music, and I wanted to go along with him. It was that swing that convinced me. I said, "Damn, I'm a gonna get in that band if I can!"

Q. What's the Arkestra's influence on the Jazz scene today?

A. We're taking what he gave us, presenting and changing it, and moving on. Like someone used to say, "everything is not finished; there always more to do." As the Arkestra's leader, I'm just trying to keep the band and its integrity intact, play tunes that everybody knows and some that Sun Ra didn't play very often. He had many styles too, so that gives us a lot of flexibility. We also use every instrument that was ever invented, and some we knew very little about: we've played on Chinese and Hawaiian instruments - "strange strings!", we used to say...from Morocco and Japan.

Q. Sounds like you still feel his presence?

A. His presence will never be lost, though I'm not the genius he was and is. By feeling his spirit, I don't have to say a word.

(top) - Sun Ra by Ramsess.
(bottom) - Marshall Allen, stage front right.

Q. Who were the musicians who accepted your French horn into their midst?

A. Around 1976, I joined Sun Ra's Arkestra and a year later went to Africa with the band. In 1978 I started working with Carla Bley's band and that lasted for six years or so. Around the time I left Carla's band, Lester Bowie was forming his Brass Fantasy band and I started working with him: there was a lot more freedom with Lester and the music was more inventive; thirteen years later, I'm still working with him. I also have my own group called "Next Mode".

Q. Tell me about Sun Ra's band?

A. That band has been around for 48 years. I think Sun Ra was one of the most incredible minds of the 20th century, along with Einstein and a couple of other people. I was on the road with him, worked in his band for three years constantly and fifteen years after that, on and off, and have the greatest admiration for his mind, as a thinker and a musical composer. From the hundreds of hours on planes and buses talking to him, I was able to learn so many things about life...and cosmology, of course, and so many different facets of music; he was like a musical encyclopedia from 1920 to the year 2000. In his band, you learned how to play in all styles: you'd take a solo and have to play like you hadn't lived beyond 1934; if you didn't, he'd give the solo to someone else.

Q. Sun Ra's shows were always a spectacle...

A. We called it multicultural because Sun Ra used film, singing, music, dance, philosophy... Sometimes he would open the performance by coming on stage and saying, "Some call me Mr. Ra, others call me Mr. Ray, you can call me Mystery!"

Q. Did Sun Ra tell stories?

A. Yeah. He once told me the most amazing story, I hope I can remember it right. It seems that he was playing a solo concert in some small town in Indiana. At the end of the show this man came up to him and said, "You moved me so much, I want to give you a token of my appreciation." He then handed Sun Ra this perfectly smooth, round stone. Sun Ra took the stone, put it in his pocket, went back to a 5th floor apartment provided by the concert promoter; and put it on the night table next to the bed. As soon as his head hit the pillow, he heard this man and woman screaming and fighting above him. The noise kept getting louder, and next thing he knew, he could see their silhouettes coming down the fire escape right outside his window. "What kind of a building is this?", Sun Ra wondered. The noise didn't stop and he couldn't sleep, so he took the stone from the table, went out into the hallway, and threw it down the stairwell. When he got back into his room, the noise and fighting had stopped.

The next morning, he told the promoter what he'd seen and heard. The promoter asked where and Sun Ra said "upstairs!" The promoter said, "But this is the top floor, there's only the roof above." Sun Ra said, "But, I saw them come down the fire escape, they were right there fighting!" The promoter ushered Sun Ra over to the window and, lo and behold! there was no fire escape. Sun Ra and the promoter then reflected, "That must have been some stone!"

Q. Do you have a story about the Arkestra on the road?

A. One time we were driving through New Mexico at 1:00 A.M. when Sun Ra told the driver he was hungry. We all knew what that meant - drop everything and prepare to eat. So everybody's looking for a place to stop, and we saw this sign, "Restaurant"; no name, just "Restaurant." We turned off and headed down this dirt road for a couple of miles until we saw a neon Budweiser sign. We stopped, got out and looked inside. There were eight, maybe ten redneck types in the place, sitting at the bar drinking beer, and then there was Sun Ra, standing in the doorway with his cape on, an image of the big red planet and its rings on the front, and lights spinning around on the crown on his head; the way Sun Ra dressed for the stage, he dressed in life. When the bar patrons turned to look toward the door, they all stopped moving: facial expressions froze; even the music playing on the jukebox broke off. Then all the guys in the band, wearing turbans, started filing in, but still none of the rednecks moved. Finally, a lady came over and said, "Hi, where you all from?" A chorus answered... "SATURN!"

Q. Who did you start playing with?

A. In 1976 when I first finished my studies at the university, Pat Patrick who was a teacher there said I should come play with Sun Ra's band. We went to Paris and stayed for three months: to come right out of college and do something like that was good; it was like taking graduate courses. I played with Sun Ra for 3 years until 1979, though I didn't live in the communal house in Philadelphia like a lot of his musicians did; I lived in New York and would just come to rehearsals and play the gigs. What an incredible band! All those great performers.

After leaving the band, I lived at Studio WIS - Warren Smith had his loft there on 21st Street- where a lot of musicians used to come and rehearse and even live. That was my network, and I met a lot of people. I started working with Abdullah Ibrahim and, at the same time, with Henry Threadgill, David Murray and Sam Rivers who had a very important band and a loft space at that time. That was when a lot of musicians were coming to town from California, St. Louis and Chicago, and we would be playing at (Rashied) "Ali's Alley", or Joe Lee Wilson's, or any one of a number of other lofts.

(top left) -Tribute to Sun Ra at Les Banlieues Bleues. (left to Right) Craig Harris, Curtis Lundy, Hamiet Bluiett, Andrew Cyrille, (not shown) Chief Bey.

(center and right) - Craig Harris originated "Slide Right" (4 trombones), with Ray Anderson, George Lewis and Gary Valente.

Q. How do you see the evolution of Jazz music in the nineties?

A. I don't think the music being played today, which I would call re-creation, can match the innovations which were going on when I came onto the scene in the sixties when everything was being created - 'Trane was still surging ahead; Mingus put out 'Black Saint' and 'Sinner Lady' which was all new and had never been done before and we were excited; Monk was still writing and composing - I played opposite him in the Village Vanguard when he was writing 'Green Dolphin Street', and when he was playing, everybody was dancing, Monk included; the joint was really jumpin'! And, of course, Roland Kirk was always doing something new. He would be listening to music 24 hours a day, and would say if the music didn't make chills run up and down his body, it wasn't worth playing. I traveled with him to different places all around the country and he knew all the authentic players in every city - when we'd go to Chicago, he'd look up Von Freeman first thing 'cause he was, and still is, one of the baddest tenors around in the scene. We had more fun. The musicians today study Coltrane solos, on say 'Giant Steps', like they would a Mozart concerto: they play well but don't create; it's fashionable to sound like Miles and the other greats. Back in the days, you made sure you didn't sound like anybody else, alive or dead; all Sonny Rollins or Jackie McLean, for example, gotta do is play one note and the listener knows who's playing.

Don't get me wrong! There are some musicians today, I think of David Murray and his Big Band, who are moving ahead, who have kept the spirituality in their music. We're also keeping on in Sun Ra's Arkestra.

JARIBU SHAHID bass player
AHMED ABDULLAH trumpet player

JARIBU SHAHID

Q. What style of music do you prefer to play?

A. The good thing about coming up in Detroit when I did was there were top-notch inside masters who could play any type of music you wanted to learn - Rock 'n Roll, Motown, Bebop, Swing - there were cats who were part of the thing: Marcus Belgrave, Kenny Cox and others were very charitable, relaxed to the situation and would help you.

In 1976 Farouk C. Bey formed a group called "Griot Galaxy" and that's where I eventually met Tani Tabbal. We started exploring meters and mixed-meters in the particular way Farouk wrote. We were able to execute Farouk's concept in a small group, along with A. Spencer Barefield, who had an organization in Detroit called the Creative Arts Collective which held concerts with musicians such as Roscoe Mitchell, Oliver Lake, Hamiet Bluiett, Abdul Wadud, Anthony Braxton, Leroy Jenkins... I'd say that was our contribution to the language of the so-called avant garde, as opposed to the Chicago, the St. Louis and the other great Midwest musicians.

Q. Do you have a funny story to tell?

A. In 1978 I was invited to come and stay at Sun Ra's brownstone, "The Eye of the Hurricane" in Germantown, Philadelphia. I walked in, he was sitting there wearing four hats, writing one tune, rehearsing another, cussing' out a member of the Arkestra, telling me where to set up, and eating all at the same time. He was playing a standard composition that I didn't know. He bid me to play as soon as possible. Since I didn't know the song, I asked him what the changes were, but he just looked at me and kept playin'. So I kind of thought I could hear where the tune was going and I started being more aggressive...and as soon as I thought I knew what was happenin', that's when he stopped! He said, 'When you didn't know the song, it was wonderful. But now that you think you know it, it's most displeasing.'

AHMED ABDULLAH

Q. When did you get involved with Sun Ra?

A. I met him in the mid-sixties on the Lower East Side, but it wasn't until 1974 that he got to hear me as a mature trumpet player. I had a gig in Germantown (PA.) with a band called the "Melodic Octet": the band's rhythm section, Ronnie Boykins and Roger Blank, had both worked with Sun Ra in the sixties. The members of Sun Ra's band are tight as family: you play in a town and if you're a part of that band, everyone's gonna come out and hear you. So Sun Ra was there, and a few months later he called me and asked if I would like to start working with the band.

Q. Did you have a chance to talk with Sun Ra about cosmic and spiritual feelings?

A. You know, Sun Ra was brilliant. When you came into the band, he made you feel special. Like rehearsals, for example: he would pay your way down to Philly on Amtrak, pick you up in his big Cadillac and take you to the house, have food for you, and conduct all-day rehearsals; in the mid-seventies it was basically rehearsal time. To be in the band meant you were spiritually involved with him; he made you feel right at home.

UNIVERSAL JAZZ COALITION, INC./JAZZ CENTER OF NEW YORK
IN ASSOCIATION WITH THE GROUP

PRESENTS

THE GROUP

PHOTO CREDIT: RAYMOND ROSS

Ahmed Abdullah
Trumpet

Fred Hopkins
Bass

Marion Brown
Alto Sax

Billy Bang
Violin

Andrew Cyrille
Drums

FRIDAY & SATURDAY,
SEPT. 12 & 13, 1986

Two Shows Each Night: 9 & 11 P.M.
Admission: $10 Advance; $12.50 at Door

Ticket Information and Reservations: (212) 924-5451

JAZZ CENTER OF NEW YORK
380 Lafayette Street
(1/2-blk below E. 4th St., around the corner from Tower Records)
New York City 10003 - (212) 505-5660

Q. Why did you choose the violin and not another instrument?

A. I didn't choose the violin, it chose me. When I was about 12 years old in school in East Harlem, they picked some of us to go to a special orchestra class, and the next thing I knew I was practicing the violin. Until then, I was playing drums. When I was 8 or 9, I remember playing on the subway up in Harlem with another guy - one played the bongos and the other danced.

Q. How did you come to play in the style you do now?

A. That was my choice. When I came out of the army in 1968, I picked the violin back up again. I wanted to perform in Jazz and that was the only instrument I knew, yet since I'd been away from it for so many years, it's almost like I was starting all over again. So I began studying in a basement over on East 16th Street (Manhattan) and also took some lessons from Leroy Jenkins. I got my shit together, but I was mostly studying saxophone breathing - I was trying to imitate a horn rather than the violin, and that's how part of the style developed.

Q. Was Leroy's style then somewhat similar to what you do now?

A. When I first heard Leroy, he was with a group called "The Construction Company", out of Chicago, which included Steve McCall, Anthony Braxton, etc.; we heard them on WKCR - that was about 1968-69 - and we were shocked. What I liked about this new music was that the violin was up-front, with the saxophones and the trumpets. There was this one record store that had all the Delmark Records releases from Chicago that specialized in the new music played by Maurice McIntyre, Joseph Jarman, and many others. We were watching and studying it; a lot of guys were coming to my house to check it out.

Q. It seems to me that the violin is a much tougher instrument to master than most of the others?

A. No. I'm very comfortable with it. Many people say it's the instrument that dictates the music, but I think it's vice versa. My theory is this: if I had an old-fashioned comb, I would play with the same intensity, the same phrasing, the same attitude, 'cause the music for me is made up not so much of the instrument, but rather of all my past experiences. Even those years I spent in Vietnam! There's a lot of the war coming through my music; that would go for any instrument I'd play.

Q. Was it hard coming back from Vietnam?

A. Definitely. It's still very difficult to this day; it was extremely tough in those combat zones in 1967, and the American government didn't exercise any intelligence about the ex-soldiers. I was twenty at the time, but there were no re-entry programs to help us readjust, so my re-entry was radical. I really suffered - my girlfriend got pregnant before I went away, so when I got back, I had a daughter I didn't even know about. I didn't know how to talk to my girlfriend anymore either; it's like she had given up on me. I was shattered, totally destroyed.

Q. How did you get back into the music?

A. I was coming home to play with John Coltrane's band, but he died while I was in Vietnam. He was my only hero, musically, and there was nobody I wanted to play with. Jack Jackson was trying get me into Sun Ra's band, but that choice represented too much strictness, too militarized - it looked like the army I'd just gotten out of. So, I decided to be a leader.

My first gig was in 1974 with the bassist Earl Freeman - the record was called "Fantasy for Orchestra", and Zane Massey, Andy Carter, William Parker, Paul Chambers, Charles Burnham and others played on it. My first date as a leader was in 1975 on a record called "Survival", with William Parker, Rashid Bakr and Henry Warner: I did some of my poetry on that and, as a matter of fact, I've written some verses recently and was the featured reader at a recital just two weeks ago.

Q. How and when were you acknowledged as one of the avant garde musicians?

A. In the sixties when I first recorded my 'ESP' record, many people fell in love with my music on first hearing; they must have realized that I had something special, and that gave me a chance to do things, like traveling throughout Europe and the U.S.A.

Q. How did you get into painting?

A. That was an accident. I started painting during a tour of Italy in 1981. One day, I was bored, sitting at an outdoor cafe, and I had the urge to draw a cathedral. I liked it, kept doing it, and developed it.

Q. Do you see a link between the two types of art?

A. I think one thing that links all art forms is content and style and my style, whether I'm painting or playing sax, is the same. My style in art is the beauty of the line and the movement of the breath. I work in the oriental style.

Q. In view of your recent illness (brain aneurysm), are you listening to much Jazz music these days?

A. Hardly at all. But I know there is one great young man on the scene - .James Carter. He's a fantastic saxophone player. I went by to hear him one night at the Blue Note. It was right after he had finished playing a beautiful solo and he took the microphone and said, "Ladies and gentlemen, I understand that Mr. Marion Brown is in the house. Where are you brother?" And when I stood up he said, "I want you to know how happy I am that you are still with us." Then he told the audience about what I'd done, with Archie Shepp, Coltrane and under my own name, and then said, "The truth is, ladies and gentlemen, that we are here tonight talking Jazz like him!" Then, the band marched off the stage and came over to my table, and we all shook hands. I told James that, in my opinion, 'He's the man!' The 21st century belongs to him.

Q. Have you an amusing story connected to the music?

A. One I can tell you: the first time I played in Switzerland, I met a man and his wife at intermission. The man shook my hand but was looking at me in a very strange way, kind of threatening. Anyway, about a year later, I went back to play in Zurich. There he was again, and he said, "You know, the first time I heard you play, I was thinking about killing myself. But when I saw your eyes and heard the beautiful music that you play, I said to myself, "If Marion Brown hasn't killed himself, then I won't kill myself!" I asked him why he was feeling so bad, and he replied that he was a college professor who couldn't teach the truth but, rather, had to teach lies.

(top) - "Afternoon of a Georgia Faun" - Marion Brown: Woodcut by Steve Hannock.
(bottom) - "Buck and Bubbles" Drawing by Marion Brown.

Q. Why is your sound so different from other bass players?

A. I believe in mixing everything together, and I was fortunate to have some good teachers as I was developing. Back in Chicago where I grew up, the high school band leader, Captain Walter Guyot, one of my mentors, a very gruff old guy, a smart man, asked me what instrument I wanted to play, so I told him, "CELLO". His response was, "We don't have no cello here, this is a concert band. No, you're gonna play bass." He scared the shit out of me so I said, "Okay!" The first sound I heard that I played on the bass went all through my body, and I knew this was it. I've been playing it ever since.

Q. Was there a particular musician who influenced you?

A. I remember the first time I heard John Coltrane because I was playing traditional Jazz, and I wondered how this guy could play so much music on one chord. That started my own investigation into personal freedom. Since I'm part of the rhythm section, I started to expand rhythmically. I can do anything I want with beats, and then I add notes on top of it. And, of course, I like to break the rules. Some musicians are recording artists and some are performing artists. I'm a performer: when I'm on stage, I like to have fun. (Laughs) Sometimes, with my bow I stab the trumpet players in the back...on purpose. Or, I'll lay the bass down flat on the floor and play because so many people think it's got to be played upright, European style - no smiling, no messing around. But, music should not be so serious.

Q. What do you think of the so-called 'contemporary' Jazz?

A. Intellectual stuff!

Q. Is it still Jazz? It's not swinging, it hasn't got rhythm.

A. Much earlier in my career, I played with my favorite band of all time called Air, A-I-R, with Steve McCall and Henry Threadgill. We stayed together for ten years. That was my prolific learnin' time 'cause I learned to use my bow on the bass. We would play old music, new music, or no music at all. I played cello once, even though I had no skills.

The thing with intellectual music is that you have to have emotional musicians who play it. For example, you can play a beat so slow that you won't hear a pulse, but the musicians will have the pulse inside them. If they play well together, the audience will stay with them. But, the music industry has fucked it up. Basically what they do, they break up a good band rather than have a group of very good musicians playing together for many years which makes for a very specific sound. A band creates its own sound; you can't bring just anyone to play. A lot of the abstract, non-rhythmic, and unusual harmonic music does not work because they don't have the musicians to play it.

In my band, and any band in which I have influence, I always suggest that we play one piece of traditional Jazz, so that people can relate to what they heard years and years ago. You can write the harmonics and rhythm sections, there's nothing wrong for an artist playing music that was considered great. Traditional Jazz was, and still is, a very great art form, but people who are modern improvisers are sometimes afraid to do that... I personally don't have the slightest idea why. I enjoy playing it - Duke Ellington, Count Basie, Miles Davis. Not all night 'cause that's not what I do.

The realization hit me a couple of years ago that I never know when will be the last time I'm going to perform. So every time I play, I play as if it's the last time. A good example of that happened when I was on a tour with David Murray, John Hicks and Andrew Cyrille. We were in a kind of isolated part of Switzerland in the summertime, so I got on this bike and took a ride into the forest. But I got lost and arrived at the gig about fifteen minutes before performance time. The guys were telling me to calm down, that everything was cool, but I was all wound up and couldn't relax. We started playing and I heard John banging on the piano, real avant garde-like, to my right. David, who was in front of me, turned around, came back to where I was, took my sheet music and turned it right side up; I had it upside down and was playing it that way.

Imaginary conversation
Vincent Chancey. "Hey Fred, whadda we play next?"
Fred Hopkins. "I don't know, man, it's your gig!"

Q. I know you played with Cecil Taylor?

A. Yes, in the mid-sixties, though I met him well before playing with him. I had been playing with BaBa Olatunji, which is where I learned a lot of African rhythms. I was the only trap drummer in the midst of all these hand drummers who were playing the African rhythms that Olatunji taught.

Q. Didn't you study with Max Roach?

A. No, but through a friend of mine who knew Max, I got to talk with him about the music. The person I became very close with, though, was Philly Joe Jones - he'd take me to recording sessions he did and let me sit in with musicians he was playing with, like Cannonball, Coltrane... So, it was quite an experience.

Q. I know you have a Haitian background, though you were born and raised here. Do you think that African drum background has helped you find your unique drumming style? I know that the African drum has more to it than just the beat and the rhythm...

A. You mean rhythmic tattooing. Yes, that's true. If you listen to a lot of the older drummers, like Baby Dodds, Jo Jones, and maybe even Chick Webb...well, people like Zutty Singleton, maybe Sid Catlett, who would play tom toms along with the snare drum. The difference is obvious: a snare drum has "snares" or "strands" that were once made out of cat gut, but now are made of wire: tighten the snares and you get a vibration and high, very treble-like sound; disengage the snares and you'll get a sound like a tom-tom. In addition to the snare drum, drummers started using drums which they'd tune to different pitches, and this meant they would be getting a sound something like a drum choir in Africa, where three or four drummers would be playing different sounding drums. Here, we'd have a drum set with each drum tuned to a different pitch, and that way you could begin to make a melodic sequence of sound as you're playing rhythm. When you talk about that in terms of Africa, there's a very direct link.

DENIS CHARLES (1933-1998) drummer

Q. How long have you been playing?

A. I started here in 1954, but I was playing as a kid in the Caribbean: I was born in St. Croix, Virgin Islands, and my grandfather and father were musicians; I was in a band when I was seven, playing calypso. When my mother and father separated, I came with her to Harlem after the war in 1945. At the time, there was nothing but Bebop being played. I didn't play Bebop, but I absorbed it. I heard Dizzy, Charlie Parker, Miles, Fats Navarro, Art Blakey, Max Roach, Roy Haynes...all of them. Then, in 1954 I met Cecil Taylor and made my first record with him and Steve Lacy in 1955. After that, though, I stopped for ten years when my first wife died, but then I got back into it again through my younger brother who also plays drums. The great flute player, James Newton, talked me into playing again.

Q. Who have you been playing with recently?

A. I've got a French connection. There's a group in Paris called "Outlaws in Jazz" - Didier Levallet (bass), Daunik Lazro (saxophone), and Jacques Berrocal. And I'm playing with Joel Forrest, a very great piano player, with Dave Hollister on bass and Claire Devitt on baritone; we play all of Joel's original music. Whoever calls me, I'll play with, or I'll do my own thing sometimes.

Q. Have you a particular drum style?

A. I've opened up my head from listening to Sonny Murray, Andrew Cyrille, and Rashied Ali too, and all the other drummers who are playing so-called 'free'. I've been learning how to make sounds from my own ear. It's not just chaos, you're trying to make music out of sound; you don't have to have the beat. I guess I learned that, too, from Cecil in a way. He would say, "Just play the drums, man!" And I'd say, "What tempo?" He said, "No tempo, just play the drums!" Since at that time, I was trying to be a Bebop drummer, I didn't know what he was talking about. But over the years I've learned by listening to cats who play solo 'free', that it's just about sound in a way we never hear it. So I make sound but try to make it "sensible" sound; rather than playing something chaotic, I would lay back and play nothing at all until I hear something inspirational. You've got to be intelligent too, not just bash and bang for a hot minute! I do it but not too long. It's like weather changes- there's the hurricane, but also the calm. Dynamics are very important to me - you can play soft or not at all, or play like an elevator ride - up, loud, high, in between, you know what I mean. I don't want to be on the top floor all the time.

the fourth annual
VISION festival

* MONDAY MAY 31 *
DENIS CHARLES MEMORIAL

7:00pm   **ANDREW CYRILLE QUARTET**
Mark Helias • Greg Tardy • Andy Bemkey

8:00pm   **Dance PATRICIA NICHOLSON w.**
William Parker

9:00pm   **THE JAZZ DOCTORS**
FRANK LOWE• BILLY BANG •
Abbie Radar • Ed Schuller

10:00pm   **DRUM CHOIR FOR DENIS**
led by BILLY HIGGINS
RASHIED ALI • ANDREW CYRILLE
SUNNY MURRAY • WARREN SMITH

"No tempo, just play the drums."

Q. What 's up with you these days Archie?

A. Currently I'm teaching at the University of Massachusetts in the Black Studies Department. Formerly we had quite a fine array of teachers - Max Roach and Yusef Lateef, among others. It's been a very good environment for me.

Q. Who were the musicians who inspired or influenced you?

A. When I look back on it, I'd have to say that Jimmy McGriff had a profound influence on my musical development. He lived at one end of the avenue (in Philadelphia), I lived at the other, and one day as I came out of my house, I heard this saxophone. At the time I was playing clarinet. So I heard Jimmy playing Illinois Jacquet's "Flying Home" solo right there in the street and, as I passed, I said to myself, "I want a saxophone." It's funny, too, because Jimmy had never played the saxophone before, he just picked it up and played it.

A couple years later I met Lee Morgan, and he was quite a big influence on me as far as chords and chord changes were concerned. I remember having a discussion with my father because I had dispensed with the Blues and was getting into Bird and things like that. For people like my father, the notes in Bebop were played too fast, there wasn't enough Lightening Hopkins and hard Blues in it.

Q. Did you study music at school?

A. I went to college as a pre-law major since my father always discouraged me from becoming a musician. In my third year, I wrote a short story and my teacher commented that my dialogues were good and that maybe I should become a playwright. That turned me around: I ended up majoring in theater, and my thesis was, in fact, a play I wrote. Eventually it was played off-Broadway in New York by the Chelsea Theater Company with the title 'The Communists'.

I went to school in Vermont and came to New York after graduation in 1959. That's when I met Cecil Taylor through his bass player, a white guy, Buell Neidlinger, who told Cecil that I might be the saxophone player Cecil was looking for. Anyway, I met Cecil on the street, quite by chance, near Sweet Basil's. He asked if I was Archie Shepp and said, "How'd you like to make a record?" Just like that! That turned into my very first recording date, a record called "The World of Cecil Taylor".

So, that's how I got into so-called "Free Jazz" though it wasn't called that as yet. That music grew up in a certain ambience. I mean Cecil and Dave Amram had opened up "The Five Spot" before Thelonius Monk came in, and then Cecil decided to bring Monk in because he had a bigger name; in fact, it was Monk who stayed on for a year or two and made the club.

Q. How would you describe the music you yourself are playing right now?

A. Let me say this. In the 60's through the good graces of John Coltrane, I was able to get a long term contract with Impulse Records: it wasn't very lucrative - for example, it didn't keep me and my family, six of us in all, off of welfare. But what it did enable me to do was get the very best musicians, like Roy Haynes, Ron Carter, Willie Shaw and Howard Johnson, as well as composers and arrangers available to play on my record dates. So, as far as I'm concerned, each of those Impulse recordings was a work of art: I had money, I could think about it, and I could rehearse my band - everything that I have been unable to do since then.

Now, I work for a company that gives me four, maybe five hours in the studio. For them, time is money, so it's really not possible for me to create on that level. An average Rock & Roll band may get six months in the studio and see the record released in two weeks, on the one hand, while a Jazz band will get six hours in the studio and have to wait a year for the album to be released.

You know, Blacks playing in the abstract are not as interesting as Blacks singing and dancing; that goes back to the minstrel show. I know that my mother, bless her soul - she's dead now - would come and say, 'Honey, you still playing those songs that got no tune?' I guess that sums up the avant garde for a lot of people. Black people themselves prefer to see an MC Hammer, with an occasional saxophone solo, than listen to Charlie Parker or Monk, no matter how great the latter solo, 'cause they can get up and dance, they can sing along - they're totally involved! This is something which is intrinsic to perform- ances of Negro instrumental music that will never be accepted on a popular basis like Negro song and dance.

For myself, largely because I've gone through an avant garde phase and distanced myself from it, I'm much more interested now in Afro American Blues idioms, and dance too: they're much more explicit and specific and direct, and reach people, So in the seventies, I tried to move back to the roots and, today, I'd say I'm 100% back in the Blues. At least, everything I do has to swing, else it doesn't make any sense. I think Coltrane summed up what avant garde music could be about...

I haven't used the term 'Jazz' because I don't make a separation between the different phases of historical African American music, such as "Blues" music, so-called "Rock & Roll" music, so-called "Hip Hop" music - I would make no differentiation between John Coltrane and James Brown; for me, James and John are the same. All of this is part of a historic continuum which has been egregiously, arbitrarily and systematically separated by the creators of musical fiction, so- called Jazz critics who make their living talking about Negro music...

Q. Do you have a funny story to tell?

A. One night at the Village Vanguard, Thelonius Monk was playing, with Pat Patrick - who's dead now - on tenor saxophone and Wilbur Ware on bass. I arrived around 10:00 - 10:30, and Wilbur came over and kinda pulled me to the side and said quietly, "Archie, take your horn out, Monk doesn't want to play with anyone. When Pat announced that we were going to play 'Who Can I Turn To' - a popular song at the time - Monk just stood up, walked off the stage and wouldn't come back." It was true: I could hear that there was no music in the house, yet I had to tell Wilbur, "I wouldn't want to do that if Monk didn't ask me to do that." But Mr. Ware insisted and after considerable coaxing, I went up onto the bandstand and played one song, "Sophisticated Lady." When I got to the bridge, I heard this piano - he played "dee bo dee bo dee bo dee!" It was Monk alright. He played the bridge, then he got up and walked off again. He didn't play at all for the rest of the night. Rahssaan Kirk came later and played.

I remember at the end of the night, after most everybody was out of the place, Monk came up onto the bandstand and started playing "Who Can I Turn To." It was one of the greatest solo performances I've ever heard!

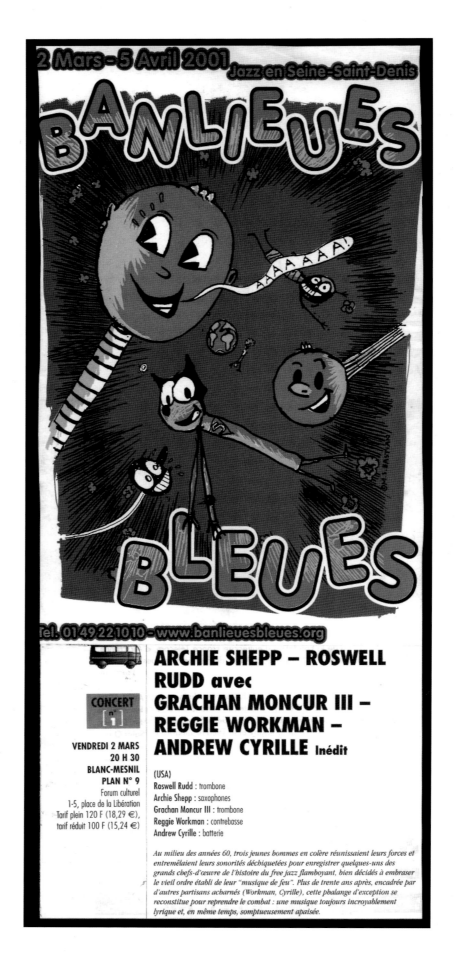

REGGIE WORKMAN bass player

Q. When did you start playing bass?

A. My last half-year of junior high school because I didn't have the instrument until then. I started playing the euphonium and tuba, but then the school found an old bass, and I started carrying it back and forth between home and school without a case. Herb Gordy, a great left-handed bass player who lived around the corner from me, played a right-handed bass turned around backward, like Earl May. His daughter was in my classes in school, so I got to know her and him, and my interest in the bass just kept growing from that time.

Q. And, what kind of music are you playing today? Contemporary music?

A. Well, Futuristic concepts! Contemporary may mean Hip Hop, Funk, Rock, Pop, everything that contemporary people are into. Futuristic means something that stems from modern Jazz and has moved on into the avant garde label. I worked with John Coltrane and his band and assimilated some of his knowledge; there's also Sun Ra, Miles...everybody, I guess. That's my concept: we have to keep one foot in the tradition and one foot in the future, in order to be really worthy every day of what society calls an artist.

Q. What do you think of this tendency in new Jazz...to be like a brother to modern, Classical music?

A. Basically, I think those guys are classically-trained musicians who were embraced by people who had money, and they were able to perform all the time because the money assured them of being in a position to create. Musicians have always been people trying to create something fresh and new, like Beethoven, Bach, Handel, Brahms; it was just in those days there were only a few styles and methods.

When you say 'brother', I would say we're traveling on synonymous paths, 'cause we're doing the same thing now they did then...but our way. Music is the result of the experience people have. Our experience, our root source and history, causes us to come up with something new now and in the future. I think that we'll never stop developing. What we call Classical music here is Jazz!

Q. Did you play with Art Blakey?

A. Back in the days when Jazz was more prominent, maybe in 1963, there was a show at the Apollo Theater on 125th St., and one of the features for the week was Art Blakey and the Jazz Messengers - of course, then, we had soloists like Wayne Shorter, Lee Morgan or Freddie Hubbard, Curtis Fuller, Art himself, Cedar Walton and myself. One of the great features of that job was meeting all the great people who used to hang out backstage. So, one time we were in the dressing room having a little party between shows. We were all having a good time, and Al Hibbler, the blind Black vocalist, walked in. There was a bottle of Hennessy going around, and everybody would be taking a drink, so we invited Al to join the party. He says, "Sure, I can use a drink." So the bottle comes around, passes by me, then by Wayne, and when it came to Al, he says, "Hold it, you just started partying, and you've already had this much to drink?" And he pointed exactly to the watermark in the Hennessy bottle, indicating how little alcohol was left.

So you could see the same thought running through everybody's mind: "Wait a minute! He's blind, so how does he know?" Several of the guys started arguing with him, thinking he was putting us all on. But, nobody in that room thought about how experienced Al must have been as a drinker; he could judge its contents by the weight. We all cracked up on that note. I would have had to laugh anyway, just seeing Wayne Shorter in stitches, considering how serious he usually is.

Lincoln Center Out of Doors 99
Dorothy and Lewis B. Cullman
Fleet Bank

August 6 – 29, 1999
Carnival of the Century
bask in the sun...boogie with the moon

Friday, August 27, 1999
Damrosch Park Bandshell 8:00 pm

GREAT MUSIC *in the* BANDSHELL

In Celebration of an African-American Legacy
THE REGGIE WORKMAN ORCHESTRA *with*
The Riverside Church Inspirational Choir

REGGIE WORKMAN, *Producer*   CHARLES TOLLIVER, *Band Director*   NEDRA OLDS-NEAL, *Choir Director*

PART I- THE CONTINUUM

THE HEALER
Nioka Workman, *cello;* Marcus Strickland, *reeds;* Dajud Delgado, *percussion*
Elizabeth Panzer, *harp;* Marla Mitchell, *movement;* Reggie Workman, *acoustic bass*

SPACES
Graham Haynes, *cornet.electronics;* Mathew Garrison, *electric bass*

PARADIGM
Mathew Garrison, *electric bass;* Dajud Delgado, *percussion;* Ronnie Burrage, *drums;* Graham Haynes, *cornet*
Reggie Workman, *acoustic bass;* Dean Bowman, *voice*

DAHOMEY DANCE/COLTRANE TIME
Odean Pope, *arranger/tenor sax;* Vincent Chancy, *French horn;* Tom Varner, *French horn;* Marshall Sealy, *French horn*
Mark Taylor, *French horn;* Robert Glasper, *piano;* Ronnie Burrage, *drums;* Reggie Workman, *acoustic bass*

SAXOPHONE SUMMIT II
John Purcell, *saxello;* Patience Higgins, *baritone sax;* Billy Harper, *tenor sax;* Marcus Strickland, *tenor sax*

CHARLES GAYLE   tenor saxophone / piano / violin player

"I'm not really into music. I don't spend much time thinking about it, but I have to survive. My sole message is: Receive Christ Jesus!"

RASHIED ALI drummer

Q. Can you talk a little bit about the evolution of jazz since you started playing?

A. I started in the late 1950's and was listening to Max Roach, Philly Joe Jones, John Coltrane, Miles Davis and Ornette Coleman. The music was changing then - Ornette's album, "The Shape of Jazz to Come"; and Eric Dolphy too. As a kid, I listened a lot to Bebop. I'd go to Jazz at the Philharmonic and listen to Coleman Hawkins and Bird at Norman Granz festivals. I got into playing via Rhythm & Blues (they call it Rock & Roll now), though I was more interested in the avant garde's new music.

I came to New York in 1962 from Philly where I had been playing with local bands. It was hard to play avant garde music there, but in New York in 1964, I recorded for the first time with Archie Shepp who was considered a Free Jazz man, having played with Cecil Taylor and John Coltrane. I also got with Albert Ayler and Marion Brown - we are all contemporaries. And, I played with Sonny Rollins and John Coltrane.

While 'Trane was alive in the 60's, everyone was moving toward the avant garde music. It went that way until he died and then everyone started switching around. That put creative Jazz on a back burner and things were pretty bad during the seventies and even up to today. But now, it seems to me that interest is happening again in the nineties. I'm playing more avant garde today than I did during the last twenty years. I guess I'm just back into this music again, and I'm playing with this band which we call "By Any Means" with Charles Gayle and William Parker where we play free form Jazz. I also have another band called "Prima Materia" where we focus on John Coltrane and Albert Ayler material.

I also have a band called "Rashied Ali's Straight Ahead" which is middle-of-the-road between the other two: this is very close to my heart since I'm playing with Ravi Coltrane, John's son, who also plays saxophone, and Matthew Garrison, Jimmy's son, who also plays bass. What a thrill to play with these kids - well, they're grownups now, but I remember before they were born. We play here, in Europe, and elsewhere. We just recorded "Meditations", which is a suite that only Coltrane himself ever recorded.

So between these bands, I'm doing really good musically. I'm also building Survival Studio, and I'm going to be working on people's records, signing people up to record, and stuff like that. I'm looking at all this young talent because I'm going to be in a position to record them very soon.

Q. Do you have a funny story about a gig, or something completely different?

A. One time when I went to France, in Royan, we were doing a record there. I had Antoine Roney, Tyler Mitchell and Greg Murphy with me, and we stayed in this old, old, old hotel. I mean it was really very old. It was so strange, and it was like out in the country. It was so dark outside, you couldn't see your hand in front of your face. And we were talking about...well, you know, we'd better be cool or else the vampires be hanging out at these old hotels. I said, "Hey man, look at my beard. There's a cross! You got to be careful out here."

So we'd all gone to our rooms and were just laying around when, all of a sudden, I heard this weird sound. I didn't know where it was coming from or nothing. So I go to my door and open it up. And Antoine, who was right across the hall from me, opened up his door at the exact same time, and we looked at each other and both screamed...!

"Would you believe it if I told you salvation is in sound, and also in the sound between the sound." Excerpt from "Music and the Shadow People", by William Parker, Centering Music

Q. I was wondering, since I've heard you play with Rashied Ali as well as in ensembles that play what I call Classical contemporary music, if it doesn't bother you to keep switching styles?

A. In order to survive in New York City, you have to play all kinds of music unless you have your own band that's working and playing one particular kind of music. So I've done what was necessary to pay the bills. Right now, I'm able to focus on my own compositions: my preference is for improvised music, what I call creative music, which is not so much notated, but where improvisation is the key. I'll organize the music for those groups that need a theme or idea to set it off, while other groups can play without any pre-set sorts; I prefer the latter. Don't matter if you call it avant garde or Jazz, just so long as it works.

I do a lot of teaching, some up at Bennington College, and also at the Conservatory. I tell them to look at music as a living organism, and when you play, it's like watering this living thing and that makes it grow. It doesn't really belong to you, even though you're playing it, since it has a life of its own, separate from you. I don't think we create music necessarily, it sort of flows through us, and we have to go along with it and know when to play hard or play rhythmically or play the melody. We call that responding to sounds, and that's what you basically train for. And when you do something long enough, you know when it feels right; and if you're good at it, you can sense when to slow down, when to break, and so on. My basic philosophy is that every musician has something to offer, and most musicians today have a hard time finding their own sound because they're not so much looking inside, but rather looking outside and trying to copy a style from the past. If your sound is like your nose, it's on you already: you don't have to look around for it 'cause it's already in here.

I think that's the idea of the whole thing, whether it's Bebop or any other music. We all use the same things - melody, harmony, rhythm. Some people say, "I don't hear the rhythm." You may not hear the rhythm because it's shifting, it's not just a constant - it's like little cells of rhythm that keep moving, one moving into another and another. But underneath the rhythm, you do have a pulse, like a heartbeat...that is constant!

There are other reasons why acceptance of Jazz music in the States leaves something to be desired. Back in the late sixties-early seventies when the Beatles were the rage, there was WBLS, a Black-owned radio station in New York City with a Black audience, whose DJ's were playing Archie Shepp, Albert Ayler, etc.; they even announced when Ayler died. Then one day in the mid-seventies, the station's format was changed to strictly Rhythm & Blues so now, there's no Black-owned station where audiences in the Black community can hear it.

And again, after the Civil Rights movement there was a Black-owned club out in Brooklyn called the "East", where you could hear Pharoah Sanders, Marvin Hannibal Peterson...on any given concert night, and there would be just Black folk in the audience listening to Free Jazz. And that reflected a growing sense of community. Politically, it had to be stopped: the music, rather than pacifying people, was deepening the sense of "negritudeness" and getting very Afrocentric.

I'd have to say 'Beatlemania' changed all that because it allowed Pop music and Rock 'n Roll stars to supplant Jazz musicians as the stars of record labels. When you think how Miles Davis saved Columbia Records with 'Sketches of Spain', and then one day he went to pick up a check and found that a rock musician was being paid five times more. Miles said, 'I'm gonna get me some of that bread', and that's how the whole Fusion thing got started. Impulse was paying John Coltrane good money until Pop/Rock came along to eclipse Jazz, and the record labels decided they wouldn't pay Jazz musicians anymore. And, at the same time that Black cultural resurgence was stopped in its tracks, the power structure began introducing drugs into the Black community and that squashed everything.

Even in the late seventies, for example, I had a job in the "SEATA Artist Program", where I would go in every day, 9 - 5, with a quartet of musicians, get paid a salary, and practice, write music for theater, dance and movies. We'd also do workshops, teach at drug centers; these were artists from all over New York. When Ronald Reagan came into office, that was cut off. So much so that this music is really underground today. I don't know how many Black people go to Lincoln Center and listen to Wynton Marsalis, but you certainly don't see many in clubs like the Blue Note.

Q. Have you a funny story or anecdote to tell?

A. Once when we were in Italy, there was a train strike. I had already gone on ahead to Austria to the gig a day ahead, but Cecil (Taylor) and Carlos (Ward) were still in Italy and couldn't get a train out. So they had to take a taxi from Italy to Austria - the promoter was getting nervous: he was happy to see them but not when he saw that big bill.

These promoters, they just want you to deliver the music: they don't care whether you've traveled from Sweden to Italy in one day, whether you've been up for 24 hours and haven't had any sleep or food and are feeling sick; they just want you to play. I remember a tenor saxophone player, Jim Pepper, who didn't show up at a concert because he had died. You should've heard the promoter, ranting and raving... "That Jim Pepper, he never shows up, I'm going to sue him. Jazz musicians are unreliable; produce a concert for them and they up and die."

SUSIE IBARRA drummer

Q. How did a woman so young get into Jazz and the drums?

A. I only started playing drums in high school, and you really couldn't say there's much of a Jazz scene in Texas where and when I grew up; there used to be a circuit in which Jazz musicians could work from town to town, but that doesn't exist anymore. The thing is, when I got to New York in 1988-89, the first band I saw and heard was Sun Ra's Arkestra. I must have been fated to play this music.

Q. What's your opinion of the Jazz scene in the nineties?

A. I see two different audiences - a Jazz audience, on the one hand, and an alternative music audience, on the other, but they're very much divided, unlike the Jazz and 'hippie' audience in the seventies that mixed together.

As far as the musicians are concerned, there are still so many talented musicians who have yet to be recognized after so many years on the circuit. But, there seems to be a resurgence, the music is going, and maybe this time around many more people will get to hear it. Still, if you were to walk around this city or other places in America, visiting different cultural venues frequented by people of different races, and you were to ask a young kid, 'Do you know who John Coltrane is?', he'd say no while in France or other parts of Europe, a young kid is more likely to know. Now that's as much of a problem as hearing Wynton Marsalis on TV telling Larry King that Coltrane had nothing more to say after "A Love Supreme". That's ridiculous and hurtful!

Q. Was it difficult for you as a woman and a Philippina to break into this Jazz world?

A. We don't have the room to publish a book-length answer to that question. It was difficult. It's difficult to be a musician, period! Wherever you come from, whoever you are. Here in the States, you also have all the social factors that are messed up - racially and gender-wise. Forget it! Together, they pose a lot of obstacles. I think sometimes that if I'd known about all of this stuff earlier in my life, I would probably have never undertaken the drums! But, I've got to say that in addition to my husband, Assif Tsahar, who gave me a lot of support, though we never played together before we were married, a lot of credit has got to go to William Parker who gave us a lot of breaks: I started playing in his big band and went on from there in other formations - like last year when David S.(Ware) was looking for a new drummer, William recommended me.

Q. Are you satisfied with the direction Jazz music is taking?

A. Yes, because it's important in many ways - it's deep, intellectual, soulful, and improvised; its present direction is also related to many forms of World Music. It's an incredible creation.

Q. Is there any comparable music in the Philippines?

A. There's percussion music played with gongs, usually in pentatonic or 7-notes scales, and swing rhythm. There's also string music, some of which has strong Spanish influences played with 14-strong guitars as well as impovised music played with a jew's harp or sung.

D. D. means "little brother " in Chinese..

A. My actual name is Robert Cleath Kanyen.

Q. Kanyen? Where are your parents from?

A. My mother is Chinese...and my father is African American.
I grew up in Canada. Yeah, it's an interesting combination and a challenge...

Q. You're Canadian, your father's Black and your mother's Chinese. How does Jazz music fit into it?

A. I started on the piano at 6, though there were all kinds of instruments - tambourines, a recorder, xylophones - around the house. I learned first by ear until I started studying: I had a lot of classical training, even throughout college at Indiana University but, nevertheless, that helped enormously for improvisation. I moved to New York in 1989 and while studying for a Master's in Jazz at the Manhattan School of Music, I took private lessons with Jaki Byard and then with Don Pullen.

During the summer of 1992 I got a gig with a big band Kit Hanrahan pulled together - Little Jimmy Scott, David Murray, J.T. Lewis on drums, Billy Bang, and others. After the gig was up, I kept in touch with most of these guys and in 1994-95, I started playing regularly with David's (Murray) various bands and Craig Harris as well. Last year, I did a tour with Billy Bang and his Bang Gang - that was a real education, the school of Bang: you learn about his music his way - he's very controlling on the bandstand and, though some people didn't like that, it's okay with me since it taught me a certain discipline. He's got this very folksy approach, like old-school, almost "countryish" violin - his style is pentatonic-based, like Irish music; but, of course, he's also got that whole "free" thing, from the loft jazz scene, and his culmination is particularly unique. So, I got my diploma from the Bang "school" and have since moved on to play with other musicians.

Q. It used to be that Jazz musicians were elevated to the position of cultural heroes of the community. Is that still so today?

A. I think that Jazz musicians who have elevated themselves and gotten proficient in their music get a certain kind of respect from Black people. I guess they think we're cool, that we have a savvy that other people don't have and a way of expressing ourselves that sounds kinda progressive.

But, Black culture is being taken away from the Black community. It's not affordable anymore; music in general is disappearing from school curricula. Back in the forties, you had people like Lester Young...the way he would talk. Graham Haynes told me a story about how Lester asked his father, Roy Haynes, to play with him. Lester said, "The slave is yours if you've got eyes!" The "slave" - meaning the job of playing drums, and "you've got eyes" - meaning if you can see yourself doing the job. That's an example of how a Black musician paraphrases a more direct way of communicating.

You know, these days all that suaveness that existed during the forties, fifties and sixties, to some extent, is disappearing. You see young players, college graduates, coming up and they talk like yuppie kids. So, that whole area of vernacular is gone.

Q. Was it your idea to get four saxophones together for the World Saxophone Quartet or had that been done before?

A. Sure, there had been saxophone sections before, playing a cappella ensemble, with Duke Ellington's, Count Basie's and Fletcher Henderson's Bands, so the idea was not new. There was also the New York Saxophone Quartet, a Classical music group, that existed before World Saxophone Quartet. But what was original and new about what we did was that we changed the concept of what a saxophone quartet could suggest: that is, four distinct individuals could come together and play music that was rhythmic - sometimes with meter, sometimes without; music that was flexible and, at the same time, had a wide range of technical things going on and reflected not only Jazz, but Folk, African and other sources. We have certain combinations of instruments that sound more "eastern", for instance, while there are others that sound more like "aboriginal" music. And I think we were the first saxophone quartet where improvisation was the main focus of the band.

Q. What about the World Saxophone Quartet with the African drummers?

A. Yeah, the fusion is beautiful. It's the individuals involved that make it so dynamic. Not because they're African, but because Mor Thaim is probably one of the top five djembe players in the world. And Mar Gueye is a great saba player and the son-in-law of Chief Bey who is considered the master djembe player. And, then there's Chief Bey himself who represents percussion from the Yoruba American side; he's the chief master drummer over here. Together we create a lot of tension and release, and it allows us saxophonists to get to the core of what it means to play with African drummers and concepts.

Q. Would you say that African music is getting into American Jazz without any problem?

A. Yes, it's more like the music never left. The African rhythms are all inside our notes. Sometimes we have to learn from them how to play African rhythms on Europeans instruments to make something else happen. And we're dealing with certain tones that are derived from European concepts, and we mix them with tones that are derived from African concepts. For example, we have embraced the South African vocal concept with the World Saxophone Quartet that kinda reminds one of the old church sound which was just a rehashing of what was happening in Africa.

Q. Have you had an out-of-the-ordinary experience connected with the music?

A. You remember that Brazilian film, "Black Orpheus", when the female lead is in the church and starts speaking in a strange tongue. Well, I witnessed that situation one time where a spirit, probably a devilish spirit, came into the church, and when it came in the door, it brought a cold wind with it. We were worshiping and it went around...went around...went around until it went into this woman and she started speaking like a man, in a man's voice; she said some very vile things to a lot of people in the church. And then, just as quickly as it came, it suddenly left the church and everybody prayed in its wake. And the door SLAMMED behind it! This whole phenomena lasted about seven-eight minutes. I believe in the power of good and evil now because I've seen it struggle within human beings in the presence of others.

Q. How do you look at the evolution of Jazz over the last ten years or so?

A. I think there's been a crystallization of groups, like the World Saxophone Quartet is one, Craig Harris has his group of trombones - George Lewis, Ray Anderson and Gary Valente. We're starting to see collectives forming, like Steve Coleman and the Brooklyn "school": people are banding together with common goals, trying to make a statement together, as opposed to the time when one soloist might burst upon the scene and totally dominate; like the way they're claiming that Wynton Marsalis is dominating as a soloist in Jazz, which is really just media hype 'cause that type of domination doesn't exist anymore in this music. There are no more John Coltranes, or Charlie Parkers; those kinds of icons are over. People like Max Roach, Sonny Rollins are two of the last ones; Art Blakey just passed, so this is the end of that cycle.

The focus of this new cycle is the group concept. I've worked very hard over the last twenty years to develop four different group concepts - my Octet, my Big Band, my Quartet format, and my Trio format. For me, it's like four different people with four different concepts that are different from one another; David of the Big Band is separate from the others so the concepts won't collide. I make so many records 'cause I've got to keep these bands playing.

(counter clockwise from the top) - Big Band at the Knitting Factory, Big Band Brass, David Murray Octet, The Quartet, David Murray.

(clockwise from top) - David Murray, David Murray, Sonny Rollins.

Q. How would you describe the music that you compose and play?

A. What I've done with my music is take the ingredients of Jazz - combustion, ignition, propulsion and heat: these are the four things, I think, which drive Jazz; the French call it "Jazz Hot", don't they? I call it "conduction." Conduction means "conducted improvisation." I use the written, notated music in combination with conducted improvisation, and you get a whole different field of music to play in where the ensemble becomes more important than the soloist. In my music, the whole ensemble solos, not the individual.

See, in a lot of Jazz bands, it's all about the soloist. There have always been great musicians, but not always great bands, though Art Blakey, Coltrane, Miles and Louis Armstrong had great bands. I think Louis' was the best ensemble band because they really played together.

So, I'm a post-Jazz musician of the nineties, like there was Bach and post-Bach. I'm not saying Jazz is dead, I'm trying to keep Jazz alive; I'm bringing something to Jazz that it didn't have. That's why I'm conducting. I'm giving something back to the music that gave me life.

Q. Has your concept been accepted?

A. I just did "Conduction #60" in Vienna last week. When I started back in 1985, people fought me and attempted to sabotage my work. But the more I did it, the more people I found whom I could trust to make this kind of music in an international community group. It's just continued to get bigger and bigger...with different people in different parts of the world - playing with traditional Japanese instruments, traditional Turkish instrument, orchestral pieces. I've even done one with the musicians of the Orchestre di Toscana whose training and backgrounds are in classical European music and who only play Brahms and Puccini, but I had them improvising. I use the same vocabulary, no matter which group or country I'm playing in: how the individual interprets that vocabulary is how the music is; how the group plays the interpretations of its members is "combustion-ignition-propulsion-heat."

Q. But does that assure communication with your listeners?

A. No. Too many times, critics analyze music instead of talking about what the music is or what it does to you. On one of Charlie Mingus' albums, he had his analyst, who'd been inside his head, write the liner notes. Critics say "Butch Morris is trying to do this or that...!" I'm not trying, I'm doing! I'm looking for the character within, I'm looking for the aura.

Q. I'm interested in your concept of "environmental orchestration?"

A. The idea is that twenty people set out with a very particular destination and a particular outcome. People want to intellectualize music to the point where there is no music anymore. Some say that what I do isn't music anymore. Why not? It's got rhythm, melody, harmony, structure and form, and this is what music is. It's also got emotion, intellect, color...

Q. Have you always played the piano?

A. It was my first instrument, and my mother was my first teacher and musical mentor - she played piano and organ for the musical groups affiliated with the church. My father was a minister and, until I was about 15, I spent a lot of time around the youth and gospel choir, going to different churches.

Around the age of 16, I started working with Little Milton who, basically, had a Blues band, but his musicians defied category and so the influences were strongly Jazz and Bebop. Early on, I had a teacher who knew Art Tatum, so I got a chance to hear him play while I was still a teenager.

Q. How about Bud Powell?

A. I actually played opposite Bud for two weeks at the old Birdland on Broadway, but I had seen him a couple of times before that as part of the Birdland All-Stars' Tour, which also featured Lester Young, Dizzy Gillespie and Roy Eldridge.

Q. Did you continue your musical studies after high school?

A. I went to Lincoln University wanting to be a lawyer. I left after two years because the music simply overcame all my other aspirations; now, I'd like to be a lawyer again so I can take care of some of my music business. After a year at the Berkeley School of Music, I came to New York and got work right away through musicians I knew from St. Louis. After a gig with Phil Woods, I went out on the road with Al Green and Billy Mitchell. In 1964 I took Cedar Walton's place working with Art Blakey's Messengers. Since then, I guess I've worked with just about anybody you can think of.

Q. How many musicians were in your big band?

A. We started out with thirteen and ended up with eighteen. Of course, I didn't mention the difficulties of keeping a big band working unless you have a situation where you can do a steady night a week; getting every musician together for a rehearsal, especially when they're all working at other things, is another problem. You need to keep a core of key musicians: even if you've got a steady gig, there'll always be some who will be in and out of the band because of other commitments; still, with the core, you can always find subs and familiarize them with the songbook. I think David's (Murray) band was so good in the sense that they were always doing new material, it was more like a workshop.

ELISE WOOD *flute player*

John (Hicks) and I tour a lot in Japan, once or twice a year, usually with a group of Japanese hosts called the New York Unit, who manage the tour the same way each time. One of the things they do, as soon as we leave Tokyo for other Japanese cities, is urge us to pack our bags lightly and put our heavy suitcases, instruments, etc. in the van. So we travel this way, making short flights and going to a different site each day where the van meets us for the gig.

On one occasion, we were lodged in a lovely, large elaborate Japanese spa. One of its customs is to have beautiful kimonos waiting for you in your room and slippers you can wear throughout the hotel. So, we got comfortable, ate well before the concert, went back to the room where our New York Unit host says, "Okay, well, pack your bags," you know, in preparation for another of these little trips, "because we'll be picking them up after the concert." So, I packed John's bag, then mine, and they came for the bags as promised.

But when I woke the next morning, I realized that I'd packed every last stitch of clothing. Here I was in that hotel, like Art Blakey would say, "I was so embarrassed!" 'cause I had no idea what I was going to do. I could go as far as the restaurant in the kimono, or to the gift shop which is where I headed desperately. I found a shirt, a nice little top with typical Japanese design in indigo blue - very special to that region. But, no pants, or skirt! And, then, I saw some Japanese-style fabric made into western-style aprons, with the strings! (laughs) So I bought two of these aprons and a little sewing kit, sat down for coffee in the lounge, and I started sewing. My Japanese host approaches, compliments me on how nice and Japanese I look in my kimono, and remarks, 'Oh, you're sewing, too!' Anyway, I kept sewing and went back to the room. When we're ready to go, I put on my new shirt and the two aprons that are now like a wrap-around skirt, with the strings tying it all together...and it worked. Everybody, except the guy who saw me sewing, was fooled: later he asked me, 'Did you buy some Japanese aprons in the gift shop?' Now, that's what I call improvisation!

Q. Did you come up playing Free Jazz?

A. When I was studying at the Creative Music Studios back in 1980, there were a lot of musicians playing that avant garde style. Frankly, at the time I couldn't handle much of it. I just wasn't ready for it, I was more into my Bebop. I understand it better today. I remember seeing Cecil Taylor in Madrid, and his music was so overwhelming: he has classical influences and African influences as well, in terms of rhythms and the way he approaches the piano like a drum.

Q. Did you integrate easily into the Jazz scene here?

A. Not really, and I'm still not really part of it. I'm from Panama and spent ten years in Madrid before coming to New York. I'm trying to make my way and consider myself very fortunate to have been able to sit in with David Murray's Big Band. I've also got a CD on Post Card Records and, hopefully, that will help me more. The album is like a World music thing, all original tunes - some straight-ahead as well as Afro-Caribbean stuff.

I also have a project which is a suite I've written for twenty-one musicians, like a double big band - two pianos, two basses, two drums, five saxophones, two trumpets, two trombones.

"Conducting the Next Legacy Orchestra"

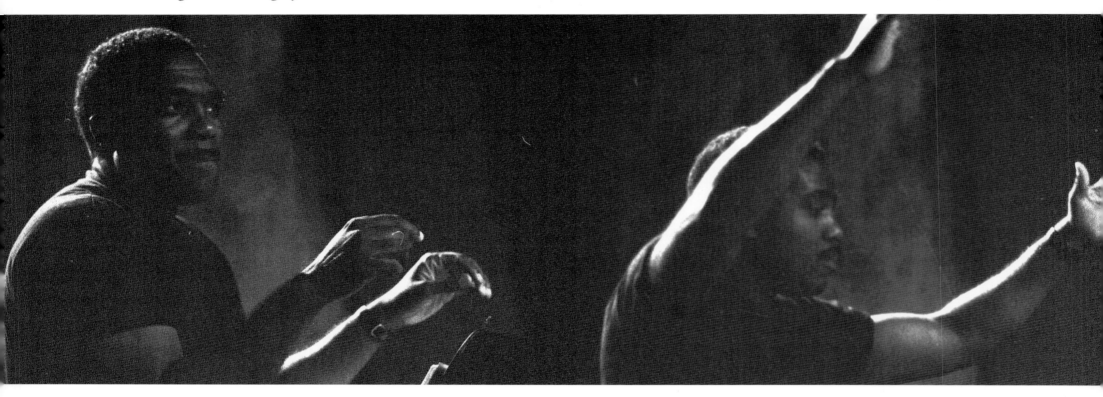

Your job as an African American has always been to create cosmos out of chaos. Our life in this country has forced us to transform harsh reality into hope. So, what happens in the course of a Jazz musician's solo is not just that musician's existence for a day. What you are hearing is the entire existence of a people who've been here in the Western hemisphere for over 500 years. You're hearing all of those ancestors whose bodies are lying at the bottom of the Atlantic Ocean. Those ancestors were speaking to John Coltrane. Charlie Parker was not allowed into the Conservatory because of the color of his skin, yet this man changed all of music forever. Why? Because our ancestors spoke to this man.

We're talking about a deeply spiritual phenomenon. If you're not spiritual yourself, the phenomenon is inexplicable.

Q. I've noticed that you move and gesticulate a lot when you're conducting. You really seem to get into the rhythm.

A. I don't really notice, but I've got to do it because Fred Hopkins never looks up and I've got to get his attention.

Q. Have you a story that reflects the spiritual side of the music??

A. In 1984, after coming to New York, I thought I was going to die. I had rheumatic fever: it's like a bacterial infection that attacks your joints, my skin turned grey, I got down to 132 lbs. I said to myself, "I've got to write this music before I die and form a big band with all my idols in it." I imagined we were at Seventh Avenue South (when it was a Jazz venue) and I started waving my arms. I couldn't have cared less since I thought there was practically no one in the audience. After the last note at the end of the first tune, I heard this thunderous applause and I thought "I'M DEAD!'" That's it, I died and went to heaven. But then it occurred to me that all those people didn't die with me, so what were they doing here? I turned around and there they were. I said, "God, I guess this is going to be it. Let it be that Your work goes on." Like I said, things always come full circle with the spirituality of this music.

Q. What's your opinion of the New York music scene in the 90's?

Frank Lacy. The last real New York "Jazz" scene was in the mid-1970's with the last of the loft concerts when cats used to have sessions: Rashied (Ali) had many concerts in his place, and others took place at RivBea which was Sam and Beatrice Rivers' place. I'm sure no one will agree with me that this was New York's last Jazz scene, and I'd have to characterize the present New York scene as conservative. Clubs like "The Vanguard" or "Sweet Basil's" always have the same groups; rarely do I see new bands playing at these clubs. The Jazz scene is international now - I hear bands in Paris or Copenhagen, for example, that play more creatively. I would even go further. Anyway, most of my work is in Europe.

Abu Salim. Many musicians, like Idris Muhammad, live in Europe and only come back when they've got a gig. For example, I live in Spain.

F.L. I don't give a fuck about America; I could make a good living not living here. You know, I've got to say it: I hate America as much as I love it! It's the racism! Everything they do comes from us. We've even changed the English language! So, why can't Jazz musicians get work in the country where the music was created? It's high culture in Europe.

A.S. America industrializes everything - culture is no more important than anything else.

Q. Can an American Jazz musician really survive living solely in Europe?

A.S. All European countries pay author's rights, but the US does not. When you join an association like I did in Spain, they track your shit and you get paid every time your music gets played in a club or on the radio.

F.L. The hippest organization of that kind is the SACEM in France: they're all together - musicians, actors, all kinds of entertainers... Like I say: Jazz is international, and this realization would make people more aware of the music and stop them from thinking about it regionally. I mean, isn't it obvious that Black music has taken over international culture: for example, Rap music in France.

Abu Salim Quartet at the Guggenheim Museum.

Q. What do you think of the evolution of African American music?

A. I think the only way you can rate music is to see how it affects people, you dig! Folk chants - you got to remember when African Americans were brought to this country, they were denied their own indigenous music. Then all the music they came up with was considered "nigger bad" music. Wherefrom comes the word 'Jazz' to describe our music. Then Bebop comes along, played by a bunch of 'dope addicts'; even before that in the Swing period they were called 'wineheads'. Chuck Berry's music didn't get on TV for a long time because it was thought that young minds would be corrupted by it. Now there's traditional music and along comes 'Rap' which is considered bad.

Q. I guess there aren't that many musicians who live strictly from their music...

A. They're far and fewer between: There are less places to play, which is ironic to me because the music is so much more popular now. Still, the fact that the music has this planetary audience has its downside too: people used to work and make it off their music when it was less popular; now, it's got a large audience in Europe, it's the rage in Japan, and there are so many other places where it's listened to, yet, there are quite a few musicians who aren't working. Though that may be because there are more musicians out there, still I can't figure why there's not enough work. Can you?

Brian Smith (left) holding forth.

Brian Smith's triple contrabass

TANI TABBAL drummer

Q. What's your opinion of the state of Jazz music, if I can use that term, in the nineties?

A. The situation today involves a battle between what I call the more rounded, creative musicians and those working with the industry to help hold the music back. What's "traditional" in Jazz is the point of change, in other words, what musicians do to change what is presently happening in the music. You see, it's all connected, and it moves forward - Jelly Roll Morton, the big banders, the Beboppers, then the sixties with Ornette and all the free music, and then the time barrier was broken...with Sonny Murray and those cats.

I grew up under Muhal and the gamut of AACM musicians since I was a kid, though I am not a member. I studied with the late, great Steve McCall for a while, and have been playing with Roscoe Mitchell since about 1978-79. I also play West African percussion, in addition to the drums, for dance classes and the Ballets Africains of Guinea. My own music compositions draw from different idioms, like playing Jazz and Blues on West African instruments and, vice versa, playing other World musics on American Jazz drum sets. I come from the Sun Ra school, if that helps explain my approach; I played with him back in the early seventies. Working with all these different bands and groups sort of allows me to see the chord that makes it all work, that links it all together. I'm always looking to answer the question, "What's the scientific core of all this, no matter what kind of music it is?"

Q. You've played with David Murray too, right?

A. I met David Murray back in 1980, but I didn't start playing with him until 1988-89, so he didn't remember that first time we met. I would see him play from time to time in between, like one time in Detroit when a musician in his Octet asked me to bring some herb over to rehearsal, and David just nodded a "hello' in my direction. Then, in the late eighties, he needed a drummer and his piano player, Dave Burrell, had him call me, and we met in Paris. At the sound check, David and I got to the stage at the same time. He looked at me and said, "You Tani?" I nodded yes, and he said, "Oh, I thought you were the herb man!"

Q. I understand that you've been with David Murray's Octet for quite some time?

A. My first gig with him was at Sweet Basil's in September, 1987, right after I signed with Muse Records, and he's kept me very busy ever since.

Q. What kind of experience is it to play with a mainly brass ensemble like the Octet?

A. Well, the music's always fresh, always different even when we're playing the same composition. The European audiences, especially, like the Octet's music; audience reaction has a positive effect on the band and that somehow makes our music different each time out.

Q. How do you like the evolution of Jazz music in the nineties?

A. There's an awful lot of things happening. There will always be something new coming out of improvisation. This music we call Jazz came out of the condition of slavery, and the music that David and I play is all part of the African continuum. Hopefully, the music will bring about some healing...for the ancestors of the slaves and the slave masters as well. We need to have a cultural understanding of who we are and how we got here.

WILL CONNELL alto saxophone / flute player and copyist
ALFRED PATTERSON trombone player

WILL CONNELL

Q. Could you explain the work of a copyist?

A. Actually, it's extracting parts - you have to go through a score and visualize pages for the instruments to play. The copyist has to have the technical understanding of the composer, that is, you have to know how to organize music just as well as the composer who created the work. There's also something called the transposition of instruments - there's do-re-me-fa-so-la-ti-do: if the note is "do", the French horn player has to see "so", the trumpet player has to see "re", the alto saxophonist has to see "la", and the alto flutist has to see "fa", all to play "do".

In fact, you might say that the copyist is the band's librarian. When you want to read a book, you go to the library. Well, I keep the music sheets for the band.

Q. That's a lot of work.

A. You see, Mozart was doing the copyist's job as well as the composer's

ALFRED PATTERSON

Q. Would you say, as a member of David Murray's Big Band, that the music you all play is 'free form'?

A. I would not like to put a label on it. Let's just say that David's band covers the history of music because of the backgrounds of the players - it's not just locked into a Jazz category. The guys play all kinds of musics - European Classical, World Music and so forth; David's playing is the opposite of a label, it goes anyplace. That's what life is about! Muhal's (Richard Abrams) music is another example of that.

Q. Do you have a funny story to tell?

A. A friend of mine was telling me the other day that he was called to do a gig, like a put-together band...quick thing, Jazz-concert type setting, I think he said 6 pieces. Anyway, one member of the group called for "C Jam Blues" as the next number. Okay, cool, he was expecting the song to be in the key of C. So the downbeat comes, the leader counts off, '1 - 2 - 1 - 2 - 3 - 4 bam!' My friend hits his first note - a concert G - but the only problem was the band was playing in the key of B flat, which made what he was playing sound like an Ornette Coleman or Cecil Taylor piece.

BOB STEWART tuba player

"Just like a bass!"

Q. How long has the tuba been played in Jazz music?

A. From the very beginning - Scott Joplin, Ragtime, New Orleans... The instruments they chose to play traditional music on were those instruments they used in marching bands, and the music has evolved out of that whole marching tradition. It's a mobile music and the only instrument as movable as a bass is the tuba. Until the movement north and semi-north in the late teens and twenties, the tuba was the instrument of choice for the bass part. Once the music was established in the North and went into the clubs, Milt Hinton told me that the tuba wasn't hip anymore, it had too much of a country aura to it, and so they started using the upright bass, playing four, slapping bass while walking (keeps time in beat box-like sound). It wasn't until the fifties when it started being used again, not as a bass but as an ensemble horn in the writings of Gil Evans and people like that. Then, since the late seventies, when I started working with Arthur Blythe, the tuba has been reintroduced as the bass in ensembles: I may have been the only one doing it at that time, but since then, a whole host of tuba players have picked up the gauntlet and are playing the instrument as a bass.

Q. Do you have a funny anecdote to tell me?

A. One of the things that helped me figure out how I should be playing tuba as a bass function was a gig I did back in the early eighties. I was very proud because this was my first quintet, I was playing bass, and I took the tape to Gil Evans to hear it. At that time, I would take it as a great compliment when people hearing my music would say, "Sounds great, Bob. Sounds just like a bass!" Well, Gil said the same thing, but put the em-PHA-sis on a different syl-LA-ble: he said, "Yeah Bob, that's great, but it JUST sounds like a bass!" He made me go back and rediscover the instrument I had lost, while technically trying to make the tuba sound like a bass.

Bob Stewart Tuba Quartet, featuring Howard Johnson (left) and Bob Stewart (right).

A. The reason goes back to the early 1600's, when the 'cors de chasse', the hunting or chase horn, was the horn that everybody played. When it became an orchestral instrument, the leading manufacturer at the time was a company named 'Raoul', a French outfit which produced state-of-the-art 'French' horns and marketed its product around the globe. The horn it produced was by far the most popular, and so it came to be known as 'French'. The Germans had their own hunting tradition and produced their own 'French' horn, a very different instrument - a much bigger instrument with a darker pitch - which came to be known as the 'German' horn. It is the 'German' horn concept which eventually took over, though today, that instrument is still called the 'French' horn. There is also a 'Viennese' or 'Veena' horn, built in Austria, which has a specific sound, and its constructor will not adapt that instrument to the norm produced elsewhere in the world.

Q. What's a flugelhorn?

A. It's a member of the trumpet family. Essentially, it's a conical board instrument, three valves, sometimes four, with a trigger. It's of German origin, historically, and was used for opera: offstage, when tenors forgot their lines or needed a boost in big opera houses, they'd have a flugelhorn playing the background - it's a darker, more veiled sound than the trumpet.

Q. Have you a favorite funny anecdote to tell?

A. In the Jazz community, you have to say 'French' horn because if you simply say horn, it could be a sax or any other instrument. Once, I was slated to do three days of recording as a horn player on a big Jazz project. I showed up for the gig, the guy looked at my French horn, and said, 'What's that?' I said, 'It's a French horn.' He said, "No, I want an English horn!" (which is a reed instrument). I lost the gig because they didn't have a French horn part.

DORIAN PARREOTT tuba

I was playing once with a circus band, called the Fun Factory, and we played one year in the Macy's Thanksgiving Day Parade. Well, it seems that the King of Morocco had seen or heard of us from that gig and so he got his Prime Minister to call Macy's which, in turn, gave him our number. One day, our band leader gets a call and it's the Moroccan Prime Minister on the other end: the Prime Minister says, 'If you get us the best circus group, we'll pay for 25 airplane tickets to fly all of them over to Morocco and back". So we spent 4 days, all expenses paid, and had a great time. We played in the royal palace and, also, at the king's daughter's estate for his granddaughter's birthday party. There were clowns as well, and when we finished in time to go play at another venue, the birthday girl insisted that we stay. She said, to the effect, "You're going to stay until I say you can go!" We had no choice...we stayed.

Q. *Have you any particular comments about African American music in the 90's?*

A. As the Art Ensemble (of Chicago) says, "You have to go from the ancient to the future!" We have to encompass as many kinds of musical forms as we can and bring the younger generations along with us. The AACM also took us under its wing - didn't matter what level you were on - which is not happening as much these days; the older players have to get back to nurturing the younger ones on the way up. I should also mention that it was the AACM which taught how to get out and market our own music, not wait for the industry to come get us.

  Take the Rap music movement - we have to jump into that sometimes so as to bring those musicians to a different awareness, to a knowledge of their roots. It's about communicating our legacy and listening to other world musics; you might call them ethnic musics, to incorporate them into our own; sometimes, audiences have to be led, kicking and screaming, into our way of thinking.

Q. *Has living in Europe meant more gigs for you?*

A. I must say I thought that's what would happen, but it hasn't. Things must have changed over the last ten years; I've been in Paris for three years now. Europe in general, and France in particular, can no longer provide us that many venues or concert dates. Maybe the politics have changed. But, a main reason I'm staying is because James Lewis, my contrebassist, one of two core members of the group I had in California for 10 years, is in Paris, and Kasim Vatumotu, a saxophonist, is in Amsterdam. I mean we're talking about 20 years of music together; and we call the group "Now Artet". I mean to get this band back together. We need to settle on a drummer and get a record deal, and I don't think I'll leave Europe until that happens.

(left to right) - Elise Wood, Rasul Siddik, James Zollar, Ravi Best.

Q. Can you describe your own sound on the trumpet?

A. For me the trumpet is a very powerful instrument, though at times you may want to be subtle with it. Clifford Brown would be my prototype and he influenced me a lot. So, in terms of my own sound, I really like to fill up the horn with explosive sounds; that doesn't mean abrasive, but I once had a teacher who told me that I should try to make the trumpet sound like a violin.

Q. How about Miles?

A. As far as sound concept is concerned, I haven't been influenced very much by him, but his musicality and musicianship are something that I greatly admire: after all, his music in the sixties influenced the whole Funk era of the seventies.

Q. Have you had formal music training?

A. I studied music at Howard University and I've had teachers, like Bill Fielder, a fantastic trumpetist in California who I still study with. I also studied with Donald Byrd and he's been like a second father to me; he believes in giving a lot to other musicians. I've played operas, shows, and a lot of different styles, like R'n B. I also played last year with Whitney Houston as well as some HipHop gigs - two with Queen Latifah. And, different styles of Jazz, not just straight ahead: playing with David's (Murray) Big Band has been a great learning experience - you can be very expressive in that style; I've also played with (Illinois) Jacquet.

Q. Where are you from?

A. Southern California. But it's here in New York where you make all the contacts. Yeah! New York has been very friendly to me.

Q. Why, among all the styles of music that you play, do you prefer Jazz?

A. This music has been so important in my life, and I'd like to pass it on to the kids, who have been mostly deprived of learning to play an instrument because of the funding cuts, the way it was passed on to me. My dad didn't play an instrument, but he liked to say he could play the hell out of a stereo. I remember when I was 13 or 14, I'd been playing the trumpet for a few years, and happened to meet Wynton Marsalis: so, as he was telling me about transcribing solos of Miles Davis and other greats, my father just started singing one of Miles' riffs right on the spot; he knew the music from records and live shows so well that he could hum or sing most chord progressions of any tune. In that sense, he kept Jazz alive for me and I'd like to do the same for the kids coming up.

(left to right) - James Zollar, Ravi Best, Craig Harris (back to camera) conducting the David Murray Big Band.

JAMES ZOLLAR trumpet player

James Zollar is a regular with David Murray's Big Band. He has also played with Henry Threadgill, Bob Stewart, Hilton Ruiz and Cecil McBee, and was featured in Robert Altman's film "Kansas City".

Q. How has your musical career evolved?

A. In junior high school in Houston, Texas, I was in a beginners' band of 25 trumpet players and was number 25 for a while. But after talking to Daryll Harper, one of the other musicians, I got to practicing and taking lessons, and right there decided that this would be my life's commitment. In high school I played in all-city and state bands and orchestras, got a BA in Music Education at Colorado State U and a Master's in classical trumpet. From there I went to the Creative Music Studio in Woodstock for a ten-day intensive program led by the Art Ensemble of Chicago - composi-tion from Roscoe (Mitchell), trumpet from Lester Bowie, music theater from Joseph Jarman, and Malachi (Favors) took us through free improvisation; the last two days consisted of a special project with Don Moye on percussion and horns.

I met David (Murray) in Boulder, CO in 1984 and became a member of his Octet and have remained part of it 'til the present. I also teach at CSU and have one class at the University of Wyoming. I had a group that won the Cognac-Hennessy "Best of Denver Jazz Search" of 1994. We'll be recording for Black Saint Records in the near future, a tribute to Sun Ra, and we'll call it "Back to Saturn."

Homage to Duke Ellington on his 100th birthday in Paris.

JAMES NEWTON *flute player*

Q. It seems the flute is not used very much in Jazz music. The first flutist who I became aware of was Bud Shank in the 1950's from the West Coast...

A. Yes, but before that you had people playing flute in the twenties, though the clarinet was the dominant wind instrument then. People in the Bebop tradition would use the flute as a backup to the saxophone...

My own playing is connected to a number of people who had a big influence on me - Eric Dolphy is foremost: his standout performance is "You Don't Know What Love Is"; it had multiphonics, glissando, and a lot of techniques that were extended, though they weren't used in a stiff way, and it has remained my blueprint all these years. Other influences have since come into the picture - Frank Wess, Yusef Lateef, and Buddy Collette, my teacher. I've also listened quite a bit, via recordings, to African peul, or flute players, who sounded a lot like another great influence, Rahsaan Roland Kirk.

So you might say that I'm always trying to put things that are old in a new environment, which is the way of African cultures.

Q. What do you think of the evolution of this music in the nineties?

A. My preoccupation with the music right now relates to spirituality. If you look at what Coltrane left behind, his statement in the cause of spirituality was extremely powerful. So, when the dignity of the song form evolved by those brought over on slave ships gets lost, the music which sustained our survival is jeopardized. That is a big part of what Jazz is - this reverence for something much greater that everyday life. Frankly, I'm not interested in playing this music unless it's addressing this matter.

Q. Do you have a funny story to tell?

A. Here's one. In 1983, I toured with Anthony Davis and Abdul Wadud. We were in Berlin, getting ready to cross over into East Berlin and get the train up to Scandinavia. But the East German border guards held up the train...just to hassle us: we had no drugs or anything else illegal, but they went through all our baggage, and all of us were furious. This dragged on for at least 20 minutes and we were at our wit's end. So, I started to pray and there came a Russian border guard, who stops to look at us. We didn't know what to expect. He says, "Musicians?" I replied "Da, da! Music." He smiles and says, "Louis Armstrong!" And I said, "Da! Louis Armstrong!" And he said, "Okay! You can go!" Thank God for Louis Armstrong!

CARMEN BRADFORD vocalist

RICKIY FORD tenor saxophone

CARMEN BRADFORD

Q. Can you give me a brief background of your musical career?

A. I was the featured singer with Count Basie's Orchestra for nine years. I've also sung with Ella Fitzgerald and Stevie Wonder. My first CD was produced in 1991, and there's been a second one in 1996 called 'With Respect', featuring Betty Carter. And, of course, I'm here in Paris to sing with David Murray's Big Band's tribute to Duke Ellington.

Q. Have you a funny story to tell?

A. When I auditioned for the job with Count Basie, I remember telling him , 'Listen, Mr. Basie, if you hired me, you'd make a lot of money; you really need a female singer.' He had a male lead singer at the time, but he said, 'Okay, I'll call you!' Nine months later to the day, on my birthday, just when I was about to blow out the candles on the cake, one of my girl friends interrupted to say that there was an old man on the phone. I thought it was a cousin of mine playing a practical joke, so I hung up in his face. But, he called right back and said, "Look, I won't call another time. Will you come and sing with the band?" When I realized he was the real Basie, I said, 'absolutely!' and two days later, I was on the bandstand in Boston.

(left to right) - Regina Carter, Oliver Lake, Carmen Bradford.

RICKIY FORD

Q. How did you come to develop your musical style?

A. Well, I started playing harmonica at a very young age. Also my grandmother was one of the original guitarists with the International Sweethearts of Rhythm, an all female orchestra which was comparable to Count Basie's Big Band of the 1940's; she would play all the standards and that got me interested in playing music as a full time professional.

Q. What's the significance of you playing Duke Ellington's music here in Paris with David Murray's Big Band?

A. One thing is that I'm playing with many musicians who are my own age. Much of my career has been spent playing with musicians who are older than me. I played in Duke Ellington's Orchestra in 1974, just after Duke died; the Band worked forty weeks that year and, as a matter of fact, that's when I first visited France.   So playing here with David and James Newton is like a reunion, and everybody is well-versed in contemporary aspects of Jazz improvisation with Duke's music as a common focal point.

Q. Have you got a funny story to tell?

A. Well, I've worked with Charles Mingus, Lionel Hampton, and a lot of other big bands. I also worked with Charles Mingus in a small unit. One night we were in San Francisco where the night before, we had played at a big university. I'd played a solo cadenza on a tune called "Sue's Chains" and gotten a good reaction from the audience. So the next night I took the same solo: I broke the solo up so I'd be playing a certain amount of phrases that I'd played the night before. Then I heard Mingus shout (imitating CM's voice), 'Don't play that again!' Then, the whole audience, about 2,000 people, started laughing. There was a moment of silence...which was when I realized I would have to play something new.

(left to right) - James Newton, Oliver Lake, James Spaulding, John Purcell, Ricky Ford, Charles Owens.

Q. *Did you start by playing the violin?*

A. Yes, when I was four...in Detroit where I'm from. I learned according to the Suzuki method which is a Japanese technique for learning to play by ear. That's given me an advantage because, even then, I had to learn to improvise, to just make up things on the spot.

Q. *That must really help you when you're playing in Muhal's (Richard Abrams) Big Band?*

A. I performed Muhal's music for the first time with the String Trio of New York which had commissioned him to write a piece. It was really something to see how the piece, written for three separate parts, fit together like a puzzle; you could play one part alone and it still made sense, like you really didn't need the other two. Then, Muhal himself called me to do this big band piece. I get to know people through the music that they write, and I could see the rhythms he likes to use. He plays around with them a lot, using rhythms that interlock with as well as oppose each other. I'm more of a rhythmic improviser than a melodic improviser, so Muhal's music suits me well: it's very challenging because there's a lot to understand; you've got to get inside it before you can become comfortable and know what he's trying to say. I wonder if the audience finds it as deep as I find it exciting.

Q. *What kind of music did you listen to when you were younger?*

A. Basically, my teacher only allowed me to listen to Classical music... I think it was only in junior high school that I started turning on the radio and hearing other things, though we never listened to any Jazz in our house. In fact, we hardly listened to any music in the house.

Still, I continued to play violin and, in my third year of college, I joined a Baroque ensemble. Playing that music was a blast 'cause there's improvising and the melodies are closer to the natural scales. There are old transcriptions of baroque music where some spaces have nothing written in - that was for improvisation. Jazz is music of the people, in the same way that baroque music was of the people: for entertainment, for dancing - popular music of the people.

(left to right) - Craig Harris, Regina Carter.

vendredi 7 et samedi 8 novembre - 20h / salle des concerts

inédits de Duke Ellington
et de Billy Strayhorn

avec notamment : *Northern Lights* (B. Strayhorn, arr. J. Newton),
Bloodcount (B. Strayhorn, arr. J. Newton), *African Flower - Fleurette
Africaine* (D. Ellington, arr. D. Murray), *Chelsea Bridge* (B. Strayhorn,
arr. J. Newton), *Warm Valley* (D. Ellington, arr. D. Murray), *Money
Jungle* (D. Ellington, arr. D. Murray), *I Love You Madly* (D. Ellington,
arr. D. Murray), *Come Sunday* (D. Ellington, arr. J. Newton), *Far East
Suite*, extraits (D. Ellington et B. Strayhorn, arr. J. Newton), *Such Sweet
Thunder* (D. Ellington, arr. J. Newton)

David Murray, James Newton, direction
big band :
Hugh Ragin, Bobby Bradford, Rasul Saddik, Ravi Best, trompettes
Craig Harris, Ray Anderson, George Lewis, Gary Valente, trombones
James Spaulding, saxophone alto, flûte
Oliver Lake, saxophones soprano et alto
Ricky Ford, Charles Owens, saxophone ténor
David Murray, saxophone ténor, clarinette basse
John Purcell, saxophone sopranino, flûte, hautbois, cor anglais, clarinette
Hamiet Bluiett, saxophone baryton, clarinettes alto et contralto
D. D. Jackson, piano
Dr. Art Davis, contrebasse
Andrew Cyrille, batterie
Klod Kiavue, percussions
Carmen Bradford, chant
Regina Carter, violon
James Newton, flûte

orchestre à cordes :
Nouvel Ensemble Instrumental du Conservatoire
Thierry de Micheaux, assistant de David Murray

concert enregistré par *France Musique*, avec le soutien de *France Inter*
coproduction cité de la musique, Conservatoire de Paris

David Murray Big Band with Strings, the Paris Conservatory's New Instrumental Ensemble,
playing the "Obscure Works of Duke Ellington and Billy Strayhorn"

*"It was very long ago
but I remember still,
the house with many many rooms
that stood upon a hill.*

*The life that was surrendered
comes to haunt us from the grave,
All in pieces, torn asunder
like the body of the brave.*

*Who used to dance
with spread wings
and wore a bangle,
and earrings...."*

Who Used to Dance, lyrics by Abbey Lincoln:

Q. What is the state of African American music today?

A. The music is not so obscure: it's like the European classical form - it's not for everybody; it's for a certain crowd of people who see themselves as artists, or identify with the arts. But I can't imagine what my life would be like without this music, because it affords me a freedom of expression and you can work to be as excellent as you can; and, the older you get, the more valuable your life is.

Q. Tell me a little about yourself?

A. It's a long story. I'm the tenth of twelve children. My father built the house I was born in while my mother was the spiritual teacher and storyteller from whom we learned most everything about ourselves. I heard Billie Holiday on the victrola when I was fourteen and grew up listening to Sarah (Vaughn), Billie, Dinah Washington and Nat Cole...

Q. Ella (Fitzgerald)?

A. Yes, she starred in the first concert I ever saw, in high school. But, you know, I never dreamed of a career as a singer. My parents let me experiment with the piano when I was five, so by the age of fourteen, I'd learned to accompany myself on a song that I hadn't studied with another person; I looked at it as a survival technique, and here I am.

Q. When did you start performing?

A. At the age of six or seven, as a soloist in school and in church, then in high school for three years in Los Angeles, and by the age of twenty-one, I was singing in night clubs in California and in 1952 in Honolulu as well. I've always had a good career, and that's why I'm so particular about what I choose to do.

You know, everybody dances our dance, no matter what they call it - Rap, Rock, Jazz...whatever! It's the music of the world. People who have music are not unfortunate. It bothers me, though, that the musicians and singers feel, somehow, that they've been left out of it because their enemy does not tell them how great they are. How can you expect someone who enslaved you to be your benefactor?

Q. What might be a first step to raise consciousness about this?

A. If the African American had any understanding at all, (s)he would restore Harlem - build a music center there and in every other neighborhood, for that matter, so that people would have to come to US to hear the music; that would stimulate all kinds of business activity. But they fight to go downtown and integrate because they have no love for their ancestors. Michael Jackson is a perfect example.

Q. You recorded a little while back with Stan Getz: you must have thought a great deal of him?

A. I love him, but you know, we have prejudice in this music as in other fields. Like in the sixties, when I was working with Max (Roach), we did wonderful work, social and all, like "The Freedom Now Suite" and "Garvey's Ghost"; Roach taught me a lot about an approach to music. But we were racist like everybody else was! We justified everything we did and cursed everybody for what they did. Today, as then, there are African American musicians who will tell you that Leontyne Price is the greatest opera singer who ever performed, yet will never even mention Maria Callas, the greatest singer that opera produced. In the same way, people will say that Stan Getz was a poor imitator; he had to go through all that.

Anyway, he agreed when I asked him to be on the album ("You Gotta Pay The Band"), even though I am reputed to be socially aware and Black-oriented... I remember back right before I recorded with him, one night at Sweet Basil's. He was sitting at a table - he had his horn with him and people were coming by to say, 'Hi Stan!' I went over to say hello and he said, 'Black... Black...Black...Black' (laughs). I went back to my seat, but I got the message. Changed my life.

BILLY JOHNSON   bass player
MARK JOHNSON   drummer

BILLY JOHNSON

Q. Billy, how did you get started playing here in New York?

BJ. When I first came, I played out on the street. I especially remember driving eighteen hours, with my bass and luggage in the car, to get here. I stayed with my sister who was married at the time to George, a saxophonist, who played with my brother Mark. Anyway, upon my arrival, George said, "Leave the bass in the car, take everything else out because we got a gig to go to." I asked, :Where's the gig?", and George said, "On Broadway! Your first gig in this town is on Broadway!'" So I said, "That sounds great, man! What's the name of the place?" Mark answered, "Howard's clothing store!" I asked, "What's the deal? Is it for advertising?" George said, "Yeah, you could say that!" So, we pulled up right in front just as Howard's was closing, and that's how I found out, to my surprise, that we were playing on the street. We opened in April and played out there until December when it got too cold. Graham Haynes and Steve Coleman, among others, would come and gig with us.

MARK JOHNSON

Q. So this is a musical family?

J. Our father, Scat Johnson, was a singer. He was from Indiana and was raised by his grandmother who had a rooming house. When musicians would come and play in the area and, you know, they couldn't stay at the hotels, they'd come to the Black part of town and find lodging at the rooming house. For example, Fats Waller used to come there a lot. When my dad was a kid, he started playing ukulele and singing on street corners to make money. Later on in life, he toured on the R.K.O. circuit doing shows, and then in the army, he started doing shows with Jack Benny and Bob Hope. Then, they used to call him "Rhythm" so when he started scatting on stage, Bob Hope gave him the name "Scat". After, he lived in Milwaukee and raised a family. He would perform around the city and in Chicago too; he wouldn't travel too far, and so even as a kid I was able to work with him all the time. He passed last year at the age of 80, but in 1994 he came to New York and we went right into the studio and recorded a CD, so I'm like a producer now. If nobody picks it up here, then I'll take it to Japan. That was one of my main goals before he died.

Q. Billy, I heard you used to work in Lionel Hampton's Big Band a while back? Have you got a story from one of those gigs?

. Everybody knows that Lionel Hampton likes to be the star of the show all the time; he has an enormous ego and, when he's on stage, it's almost impossible to get him to stop. Like, I remember one New Year's Eve, we were playing three shows at the Hotel Meridian in Paris - the first set was supposed to last an hour. After about an hour and 50 minutes, the lights got so hot that it set the sprinkler system off and everybody got wet. Lionel was scared, but he said, 'Just save the song books and keep on playin'!' We kept playin' until the fire department closed us down.

Another time, we played this concert, and Freddy Hubbard and Dizzy Gillespie were on the bill. First, we're playing Dizzy's 'Night in Tunisia', and in the middle of the cadenza, Lionel Hampton jumps in with his vibes and starts playing these chords on the pentatonic scale. Dizzy couldn't believe it. He turns around and gives Lionel Hampton a look, like "What are you doing?" And Lionel Hampton looks around and says "Chinese chords, Gates!'" You know, he called everybody "Gates." Meanwhile, the whole band is cracking up, and Dizzy never did get to play his cadenza. Lionel just conducted and ended the song.

Second half of the show, Freddy Hubbard is playing one of his songs, and Lionel Hampton does the same thing with him. Freddy got really angry. He's not as comical as Dizzy and wouldn't handle the situation the same as Dizzy. He turned around and blew the mute out of the horn right at Lionel and hit him... Pow!

Q. I understand you have a long history with this music?

A. Yes, I've been on the scene ever since I made my first record which was called, "The Cry", for Temporary Records in Hollywood in 1962.

Q. Well then, what do you think of the evolution of Jazz from then to the nineties?

A. In my honest opinion, it's a big hoax to give recognition and stardom to some contemporary "New Wavers" who are playing this music with no groove or swing; that's music without substance or life because life has a rhythm of its own which you can depend on.

So, to those false prophets preaching propaganda...beware! Music in performance must be spiritual and highly conscious...and rhythmic. And full of love! Like Duke said - "If it don't have that swing, it don't mean a damn thing!"

Q. Do you have a story about one of the great musicians you've known down through the years?

A. It was back in 1960, and I found myself hangin' out with Monk and the band. Monk liked to drink champagne at that particular time, so there were cases of a superb quality on hand as well as champagne glasses of the highest quality crystal; you know, the kind which tinkle 'Bing!' when you hit it. So, Monk would drink the champagne out of the glass and then throw the glass into the fireplace. When the glass broke, it would make a certain sound, and Monk would immediately go to the piano and play that sound. Or, he might break a light bulb, then dance over to the piano and reproduce that sound with a childish grin on his face. At the same time, he'd beat his chest with both fists, chanting, 'I'm Monk, the gorilla and the baboon.' I haven't seen anything as funny since.

MARTY EHRLICH saxophone and flute player
MICHAEL ATTIAS alto saxophone player

MARTY EHRLICH

Q. How do you feel about the evolution of Jazz in the nineties?

A. I think, as we approach the millennium, more and more people are getting away from looking at music as either supporting the tradition or supporting the avant garde. Musicians of my generation have had experience with many of the traditional forms and the different approaches of various people to the music, so I think it's a time of many possibilities, though the music business doesn't support all of them.

Q. Don't audiences expect to hear the avant garde rather than the traditional form?

A. You know, for some people traditional still means "Dixieland." Yet, part of the success that traditional Jazz is having has to do with the sentiment among the Jazz audience, especially as the practitioners of the music of the forties and fifties have died or are in retirement, to see young musicians take up playing extremely well in those styles. I really don't know whether the Jazz audience is more interested in hearing the avant garde; it's certainly not the case in America. Perhaps the reason for the success we're seeing now is that there's an audience which is not so easily defined: it's not just a Jazz concert or, even, a Rock audience; it's an audience that listens across genres, something the industry underestimates. I don't know, but I hope I'm right.

Q. How did you get involved with groups playing African American music?

A. I came to New York in 1978, but my contacts had been made before: I was part of the New Jazz scene in St. Louis with the Human Arts Ensemble and musicians like Oliver Lake, Julius Hemphill, Baikida Carroll and J.D. Parran of the Black Artists Group; and, I knew many others from attending the New England Conservatory in Boston. So, three of my first sideman gigs in New York - with Chico Hamilton, George Russell's Big Band, and Anthony Braxton's Creative Orchestra - came from among these acquaintances.

MICHAEL ATTIAS

Q. What kind of musical culture did Paris bring to you?

A. I enrolled in the Institute of Art & Cultural Perception which was founded by Alan Silva, and worked at the school's bar, in lieu of tuition, making sandwiches for Frank Wright, Jerome Cooper, Sunny Murray and others who were passing through Paris at the time. Alan's a very special teacher: on the one hand, he favors a very systematic approach — using graphs and charts and exhaustive permutations of pitch cells - - based on Schillinger and George Russell who came and taught workshops. On the other hand Alan comes out of a musical practice that's very intuitive and his classes often turned into collective free improvisations with him at the piano. Some of the other teachers there had either come up in the 1970's in the wake of the Black Power movement or were big-band musicians who'd been invited to France to form an all-star big band; the clashes and alliances between the two factions were very instructive as well. And, in the clubs I'd go see Steve Lacy all the time, standing in the doorway 'cause I didn't have the money, and got to meet the musicians he played with. I played a concert with Bobby Few. I started doing arrangements for an all-Monk pianoless quartet, studying his music intensely, and writing stuff of my own.

Q. What excites you about the music that's being played today?

A. I think it's that the different stratas of activity are allowing many musicians to move diagonally across them, so to speak. It's what has made me want to live in New York. In Paris, everything seemed musically very segregated: Bop musicians don't have anything to do with the improvisers, Arab musicians hardly ever play with the Africans, rockers don't mix with classical musicians. Here, I can learn about and play all sorts of musics, jazz, Latin, noise, classical, etc. as well as pursue my own in the company of musicians equally hungry for this diagonal motion. Eddie Palmieri's band of the 1960's was a model of collective improvisation as vital in a sense as Ornette's band in the same period. There's the strong popular tradition and, of course, the avant garde. To me, Jazz is a way of treating relationships between musicians, more than a specific style. It's a particular way people can interact and produce sound together.

Q. ...Like a family?

A. Better than a family!

"I played with Dizzy Gillespie when he came to Puerto Rico about twelve years ago and he brought me to New York City with his orchestra. That's where I live now and play with David Murray's Big Band and Lester Bowie's Brass Fantasy. Lester taught me that I shouldn't worry about people understanding what I'm playing now: the avant garde looks to the future so the audience will ultimately come to understand."

Drawing by Jerome Lagarrigue.

Q. How did you get started in music?

A. My father, who was a factory worker at a wool mill in Massachusetts, played the trombone on weekends, so he started me off when I was nine. He was also a Louis Armstrong fan, so I got to see Louis play and met many of his trombone players - Trummy Young, Jack Teagarten, Tyree Glenn; when I saw Louis in 1963, Big Chief Russell Moore was his trombonist. That turned my life around. Later, I studied with Jaki Byard and George Russell at the New England Conservatory of Music. In 1977 I moved to New York and started playing with Carla Bley's Band in 1980. Two years later, I joined Cab Calloway's Orchestra and that relationship lasted for nine years. There's no one like Cab, he's being sorely missed.

Q. Have you got a short, funny story about life as a musician?

A. Back in 1980 or '81, we were in the south of France - there were 6 horns in Carla's 10-piece band. It was our day off and, before going to the beach, I'd hung the "Do Not Disturb" sign outside my hotel room door. When I got back to my room, I picked up my horn and realized that the bell was crinkled, the top of the horn was all bent, and there was a hole in the outer slide. I was told later that two maids had come into the room, despite the "Do Not Disturb" sign, and began marching around the hotel hallway playing the horn like it was a parade. But one maid dropped it and that's how it had been destroyed.

Anyway, while still dripping wet - I'm a big, funny-looking guy too - I took the bell off and, holding it over my head, went down into the hotel lobby, screaming that I'm gonna kill somebody. Luckily, Bob Stewart stopped me and negotiated some money for repairs.

The horn was a 1935 King. When I got home, I used the money Bob had negotiated for me to buy a new one, a Martin. But 2-3 years later, I took the old King out of the closet, had it redone, and that's the instrument I'm still playing today.

(right to left) - Gary Valente, Alex Harding, Vincent Chancey's French horn.

FRANK LOWE tenor saxophone player
ANDREW LAMB tenor saxophone player

FRANK LOWE

Q. Who are you working with now?

A. I'm in a group called "Saxemble" (James Carter, Michael Marcus, Cassius Richmond, Cindy Blackman, + Alex Harding and Bobby LaVell), and also just finished a recording with Joe McPhee (saxophone and trumpet), Charles Moffett (drums), and David Prentice (violin). I'm also working in a group with Denis Charles.

Q. How did you come to be playing so-called Jazz music?

A. I started singing in junior church choir (in Memphis) when I was about 8 or 9. Then in junior high, I joined the glee club because there was this great conductor, Robert Shaw. I also had a band instructor in school by the name of "Tuff" Green: he knew Billie Holiday and Charlie Parker, and he produced B.B. King's first hit; I learned the whole Jazz ideology from him. Tuff had this great concept that was instilled in me early: there are things that pass through you, not written on paper, that cannot be bought or sold - the soul part, the hard part.

Q. When did you start playing sax professionally?

A. I made my first recording with Alice Coltrane in 1971. I had been living in Berkeley, CA., and playing with Sun Ra for about a year, studying with John Gilmore. John was a 360 degree person and, actually, did a lot of things that Coltrane got credit for; it must be "karma", but John Gilmore just did not get his due. At the same time, there was this cat named Bert Wilson, a real good, West Coast saxophone player - he's physically challenged, confined to a wheel chair, but a terribly gifted musician. Bert and Don Rafael Garrett were my teachers - Rafael taught me breathing and the concept of using the "chi", the energy center in the solar plexus that's so important in Tai Chi Chuan and Yoga, to get a good tone which is a must for listeners. I also met Ornette Coleman out there and when I got to New York, it was through Ornette that I got in touch with Alice.

ANDREW LAMB

Q. How long have you been playing saxophone?

A. Since 1975. It was sudden! The sound of the sax became an obsession. I'd be dreaming about it, so I had to get one. Once I had it, I closed the windows, filled up the orange juice jar, got a towel, and went at it. I've had no formal training, so I'm self-taught...by the grace of God. When I picked up the instrument, I knew what I wanted to do: I'd heard a little bit of everything, but Jazz music is an extension of my being and I wanted to tell things my own way. I like to sing through the instrument, tell a story if you will within the music.

Q. You have a quartet now?

A. Yes, I met Warren Smith and Andre Strobert out at SUNY Old Westbury where both were teachers - (Makanda) Ken McIntyre ran the program which was very different from the Jazz tradition, even though the tradition was also taught. Both Warren and Andre have played musics that touched so many different diasporas, it was like I could hear whole African villages playing. So when I left the program, I said to myself that I would call on them when I got on my feet. That time came, and so I enlisted them both as well as Wilbur Morris; we've been together about 4 years now. I should say that within the quartet, we have interchangeable combinations of duos and trios where different things happen.

Q. That's the first time I hear the name 'Makanda'...

A. It was given to me in Zimbabwe. I was performing and I took a break. A brother there gave me a piece of paper and said, 'This is your name'! I looked at it, went back up to play and at the next break, asked him what the name meant. In the Shona language, it means 'many skins'. I told him as a kid, my skin used to shed, like a snake.

Q. I'm told you play many instruments?

A. I play piano, bass, drums, all the clarinets, all the saxophones, and all the double reeds. I started playing the bugle in elementary school. I also sang in church, an Episcopalian church, with a very illustrious person named Louis Farrakhan - together, we sang first and second soprano; we sang alto as our voices changed, and then I stopped.

I really became committed to learning how to play the saxophone when I heard Charlie Parker. Bird would be playing at the High Hat, a club right across the street from where I was living in Boston, so I'd go as often as possible and sit as close to him as I am sitting with you now; my feet would be on the bandstand right next to where Bird was playing. I'd just be listening, couldn't afford to buy drinks, and when he'd get off the bandstand, I'd walk along with him - he was very loquacious, very outgoing, a really nice person. I can't remember talking to him, but I would know when he came into the club, and whether somebody sold him some bad stuff that might waste him for a night or two or three until he could get himself together and play over the weekend. That didn't bother me. He could be out of his mind when playing, sometimes with his eyes wide open, but he was seeing something else, that was clear.

Q. Didn't you play with Eric Dolphy?

A. He was on my first album and won all kinds of awards for it, including Downbeat's best bass clarinet, alto sax, and reed player. But when he couldn't find work here he went to Europe where he died. Had he been able to play here, maybe he could've been saved. We made a commemorative Eric Dolphy CD in France in 1990, with Richard Davis on bass and Thierry Bruneau on multi-reeds.

Q. As a teacher, how do you instill a feeling for Jazz in your students?

A. In playing, there is a flow. Basketball players have a term - 'get in the zone' - which fairly describes Michael Jordan when he scores 56 points; everything he throws up goes in because he's in the zone. This is life, whether it's basketball, surfing or music. There's a flow to each tempo. You have to make sure you can get to that spot, and that's what you should be practicing instead of playing this mode on that chord in this scale. Those are not musical ideas.

Q. It's physical and spiritual?

A. Once you move to honesty, you're in the realm of the spiritual. It's when a student plays, not when (s)he talks, that's meaningful. There's a communication that takes place when you listen to somebody, and that's how I teach.

Q. Well, why do you always hear musicians laughing so hard backstage?

A. Sometimes traveling, certain things happen and you don't think about it until later when you're sitting around and talking; only then do you realize how funny it was. A lot of times on a tour, in Europe or elsewhere, you run into people who you don't see often or get to hang around with much, and we reminisce about people we know and end up having a good time. Or we start riding each other. That's our entertainment on the road, telling stories about each other. When people come out to see us, the idea that we're working gets lost on the audience. There are times when we've traveled 4 or 5 hours to get to the hotel, then check in, then go to the concert hall, do a sound check, and then perform. After the concert, very often you're wiped out and just want to go to sleep 'cause you're going to do the exact same thing the next day in another city or town.

Q. Is there a sum total of your musical experience that you can describe briefly?

A. No matter where I've performed as a musician: several times in Japan, Russia, Europe, South America, and throughout the U.S.; nor with whom: Max Roach - we've been playing for 25 years and recorded 30+ albums, or Horace Silver's band, the Thad Jones/Mel Lewis Big Band, Duke Ellington's Orchestra (conducted by his son Mercer), the Count Basie Orchestra, the Jazz Messengers, Anthony Braxton and Muhal's (Richard Abrams) Big Band; I see that people are trying to do the best they can, whatever the situation they're living in. There have been times, as I'm playing, that I think I'm really into it, and yet, afterwards, somebody says, 'I enjoyed it but...' Then there are other times when I thought I wasn't into it at all, and yet, later on, someone'll come up and say, 'Wow, that was the greatest...' So an artist has to know when you're really on and when you're not 'cause, in both cases, you gotta do better for the next audience.

Q. When you get into the 'zone'...

A. Right! There are times when I know it was not me playing the instrument. I remember a particular concert, playing some things that I know I could not have played. It had to be Louis Armstrong because it sounded like him. Everything was perfect - I didn't miss a note, I didn't get tired, I felt like I could've played for a month; it was like time doesn't mean anything. That's what I call an out-of-body experience because my eyes are closed, I don't feel I have to breathe, I'm looking down and watching myself play.

Art Blakey liked to say that it comes from the Creator through me to you - split-second timing. At that point in time, I'm the instrument, not the instrument I'm holding, and the truth is coming through US!. Everything just flows. A couple of times, I was able to draw the saxophone player in - he played notes in between the notes I was playing, and the notes I would have played he played. We all got into that place. It was kinda scary! I was playing a blues and after 12 bars, I just fell out laughing, right in front of the audience. It wasn't hilarious funny, but everything just fit right. That's the level I'm always trying to get back to.

JACKIE MCLEAN   alto saxophone player
ERIC MCPHERSON   drummer

(left to right) - Milt Jackson (vibes), Jackie McLean (altosax), Donald Byrd (trumpet).

Q. Do you think that the radicalism of the late fifties/early sixties influenced your sound?

A. (J.Mc.) I think what influenced me to move onto a free sound was the time I spent with Charlie Mingus. I joined his band back in 1956-57, and he always wanted me to move away from Charlie Parker's style and play something that was mine. It was hard for me to think about and work on that, but ultimately I acquired my own tone. You know, I had also heard Sun Ra in 1957 in Chicago, and I've got to say that he had a great influence on me too

Q. Do you think the music which evolved during the Civil Rights era reflected what Ben Sidran calls the 'Black talk' of the community?

A. (J.Mc.) I think musicians just naturally express their environment and the world they live in. Like in the sixties, there was a lot of turmoil - the assassinations of John F. Kennedy, Malcolm X, Martin Luther King, Jr., and Robert Kennedy: it was a very violent time and people were hollering and screaming, and the music was like that; the music I was playing in 1963-64 was very open and free as compared to six or seven years before.

Q. Eric, would you say that the music you're playing today reflects the voices of the community?

A. (E.Mc.) I don't know whether my music reflects what the community is saying, but whatever time you're living in, that's naturally going to come out in your music. I grew up with Hip Hop and 'breaking', so that's where I'm at, but there has been a lot of music that has come before today, and it takes a while for young people to absorb all of this and interpret it in our own kind of way.

A. (J.Mc.) I think that's evident in Eric's playing: unlike back in the forties and fifties, he's got a lot of polyrhythms and a lot of different things going on in his expression on the drums, so his playing does reflect the time he came up in. He's a real musician.

Q. Archie Shepp told me that many Black students in the classes he gives at the University of Massachusetts don't know nearly as much about Duke Ellington and Count Basie as they do about Martin Luther King, Jr. Is this also true of your students at the Hartford School of Music?

A. (J.Mc.) Absolutely. Many students don't even know who Charlie Parker is! I make sure that in my history class, I take them all the way back in order to give them some idea of Africa's place in world history rather than as just a place where the capitalists went to get slaves. I think both Eric and Abraham (Burton) have a very broad scope when they think about music.

Q. Jackie, I read in Miles' (Davis) 'Autobiography' [As Told to Quincy Troupe] that in 1952 during a club date that you were playing, Charlie Parker was in the audience and that after the show, he expressed his enthusiasm about your playing?..

A. (J.Mc.) Yeah, I was twenty and he was thirty-one. He came over, hugged and kissed me on the cheek, and complimented me on the music.

(top) Abraham Bourton, (Bottom) Eric McPherson.

Q. *What do you think about the evolution of Jazz music in the 90's?*

A. There's a lot of great music being played, when it gets away from the corporations that are trying to push all these young Black guys with suits on us, and all the bullshit; you can't play sounds of the fifties and sell that to a 19 year-old today! You know, I look at these young musicians, like Wynton Marsalis who's such a Jazz fanatic. I wonder what kind of music he listened to when he was coming up: he's too young to have danced to Louis Armstrong

Don't believe the hype, there are some really good things going on. I've played all kinds of music - avant garde, big band, Bebop. There's a sound for every decade and what's excited me over the last several years is there's a lot of rapping and Hip Hop, Acid Jazz and so forth. You know how kids love to dance, and if we can bring that back into Jazz, that'll bring young people into being curious to know what this music is about.

Q. *Jazz hasn't been about dancing for a while?*

A. In the mid-1950's/early 60's, Jazz got strange and moved into small clubs while the big bands weren't around anymore.

Q. *And you didn't find any Black people in those clubs. There were only white people.*

A. I've been working for the last ten years or so to put together a group of rappers and dancers and do a whole production thing: it'll still be Jazz - spontaneous improvisation - but it'll be more produced, more like what Duke Ellington and Cab Calloway used to do as entertainers, with tuxedos and so forth. That's my favorite kind of Jazz. Count Basie had an enormous influence on me. So I want dancing, production numbers, costumes...the whole thing, that's what I'm into.

Q. *Do you have a funny story to tell?*

A. I was playing with Stan Getz at a gig in Washington, D.C., and we were between sets. This guy comes up to the stage where I was rapping with the pianist Andy Laverne and says, "Oh, I just drove here from Georgia (or somewhere), it took me 24 hours and I'm one of Stan Getz' biggest fans and I'd really love to meet him. Where's Stan?" We both pointed toward the dressing room and said, "That way!" So the guy proceeds to the dressing room, doesn't knock and just walks in. Stan was there with a woman - I don't know what was happening, but when he sees this guys he says, "Get the fuck out of here, you asshole!" Well, the guy backs out of the room, closes the door, and as he passes close to where I was, Andy Laverne says to him, "Nice guy, huh!"

Does scoring a piece of music for orchestra present difficulties?

Writing things out is only a barrier if you're not able to convey the music on the paper. If there's a
oblem with the medium, you've got to overcome it. One of the great things about an orchestra is
at not only are there 50 or so instruments, but 50+ musical minds. When you hear a live band,
ere's a certain interaction between the bass player and the drummer that can't be replaced by any-
ing else - good, bad or indifferent; a meeting of the minds takes place and something special hap-
ns. You have to have faith that you can make that 'something special' happen again. If you
quence something, as in Rap music, the good news is that it will come out exactly as you planned
the bad news is that it will come out exactly as you planned it since no one else will inject a musi-
l thought into the mix. If you sample something, there may be many musical thoughts, but there
n be no flux. When you have live musicians, there is that chance that they will not respond the way
u want them to, but there is that chance that they will produce something incredible. I've been
essed to be around the greatest musicians in the world because there have been times when they
ve done something incredible which has worked for me.

s an arranger, I'll work with Lester Bowie anytime he has a special project or something intricate
r which he needs a special slant, like the Prospect Park performance (in the summer of 1995) of the
ipHop Feelharmonic.

. Was it difficult arranging music for thirty instruments?

. That part's never hard. I listened to a tape of several of the artists and kicked it back and forth with
ester in order to understand what kind of a sound he was looking for; then I finalized the instrumen-
tion. The hardest part had to do with the rappers and trying to adapt the music to their situation. I
ould have felt better if I'd had the opportunity to talk to them before finalizing the arrangement; the
me element made that impossible. For example, as soon as I know how many bars this or that rapper
eeds, I can go ahead and complete the arrangement.

. Is it harder to arrange the music when Jazz musicians and Rappers perform together?

.. All music has the same basic elements of tension and release. Everybody creates tension different-
. When you sing a scale, you imply the use of certain chords which I can figure out just from listen-
g to you; so I add tones to give a roundness to the music. I must also anticipate when a certain ten-
on or release is required before proceeding to the music's next section: for example, if more rhythm
oming from the orchestra is required, then I would listen for the beat and orchestrate the drum - the
ottom of the orchestra would act as a bass drum and the middle part of the orchestra would act as
e toms; then I might decide to make the trumpet(s) act as a snare drum with tight intervals for maxi-
um impact; then take the French horns and trombones as my high hat (cymbals). Many times, you
an't get wrapped up in hearing just what's there, you have to look past that. As an arranger, you have
be able to hear what can be as opposed to just what's there.

. Do you have a funny story to tell?

. One of the most amazing things I ever saw happened when I was doing a Broadway show called
The Mystery of Edwin Drood". The way the show was set up, every night the audience would vote
who the murderer was: each character had a special theme music associated with his or her role, and
ach confession would have an orchestral number, like 29-A. One particular night, the orchestra's got
he murderer's theme music ready to play, but the guy who announced who had been voted the mur-
erer didn't have his head on straight and got the murderer wrong. Luckily, the conductor was alert
nough so that when the announcer presented 'John!' as the murderer, the conductor said, 'No, it's the
Reverend such-and-such', in a real loud voice and gave the right down beat. So everything came out
ight, but what if he hadn't had the presence of mind?

Earl McIntyre conducting Lester Bowie's HipHop Feelharmonic at Prospect Park Bandshell, Brooklyn.

Q. In your opinion, who are the Jazz singers?

A. For me, a Jazz singer is Ella Fitzgerald, Betty Carter...In fact, I'm now trying to do that traditional Jazz thing - 'cause now it's being called "traditional" - since I've always "scatted". When I moved to New York, I was like Betty Carter's shadow. So I would say that I'm probably a combination of a Betty and an Ella and Sarah Vaughn and, maybe, a little Billie Holiday in my stage approach.

Q. True, but I saw you perform live in Paris recently, and you bring another dimension to the music.

A. I'm a frustrated musician. I always wanted to be like them and be respected by musicians. I guess it stems from wanting to have the respect of my father, Matthew Garrett, a trumpet player and teacher, and from his students at Manassus High School (Virginia) — George Coleman, Phineas Newborn, Booker Little — and from Cecil (Bridgewater), my first husband...maybe. I never read music or played an instrument, the only thing I had was my voice. So I think my whole hang-up in trying to prove my musicality has been to use my voice like an instrument. That's what I do with the music of Horace Silver, for example: backed by a quintet which is the formation that is usually associated with Horace's music, my voice is the 6th instrument.

My approach to Jazz stems from the four years I spent with the Thad Jones/Mel Lewis Orchestra, the way Thad would always give the trumpet section a riff to play behind someone who was doing a solo. And then, me working with Dizzy Gillespie and Clark Terry, that's what they did too. So I'm just an extension of my experiences with different musicians I worked with, and I guess what I'm doing in the 90's is going back and finding where I left off in the 70's. So I don't think I'm doing anything special... (laughter). A lot of singers in the 80's were doing original material to create their own style, so that no one would associate them with anyone else. When I came out with "Keep the Tradition", nobody was really doing standards, but now there are all these "standards" albums.

Q. Would you have a funny story to tell?

A. There's a friend of ours who's done a book of funny stories about Dizzy Gillespie. In 1985 I was in Nîmes (a French city in southwestern France) for a Jazz festival and had just checked into the hotel. I get my key and go up to my room. The door to the room next to mine is wide open, so I say to myself, "Oh, I wonder who that is?" I'm putting the key to the lock of my door when this man, in his shorts and a sleeveless T-Shirt, comes to the open doorway. It was Dizzy and he says, "Mooshy wooshy, baby! My door is open, I heard you were checkin' in. I've been waiting for you to get upstairs..." That was funny!

Q. Would you mind if I asked you to talk a little bit about your father's career, in the sense of where Jon Hendricks got this idea to put lyrics to Jazz music?

A. I'm not sure how it came about, but I think I know what Dad would be thinking: I myself write lyrics and, very often, I'll hear an instrumental and, to me, it just needs to be sung. He still does it today, it's amazing how he writes lyrics. He'll listen to a song, pick up a note pad, start writing and, fifteen minutes later...Boom! It's a song. So spontaneously! Like he's speaking! Being a drummer helped him a lot, for the rhythm, word stress, and the language

Q. Had he been part of a Jazz group at the time?

A. He was playing locally in New York and studying law; he had a year or so to go before taking the bar exam, but he gave it up for Lambert, Hendricks & Ross. It was the recording, "Sing a Song of Basie", which launched his career. Apparently, it was their plan to record those tunes with a chorus Dave Lambert had called the David Lambert Singers, of which Annie Ross was a member. But, they didn't like the sound of the bigger group and, instead, used

only three voices and overdubbed the parts. So, this was a very innovative record for many reasons - it was the first time 'vocalese', so to speak, had been done for solos, backgrounds and band arrangements, and the first time overdubbing had been used to such an extent. It was extremely successful.

You know, they did a second album, this time with the Basie Band, and after that they would find songs that they liked - Ellington compositions, Horace Silver tunes...

Q. Are you familiar with the group "Double 6"? I mean, they did what Lambert, Hendricks & Ross were doing, only in French using Charlie Parker's music, for example.

A. Oh yeah, Mimi Perrin. I think what she did was fabulous.

Q. Especially because it's so difficult to rhythm the French language to suit swing music.

A. I do a lot of teaching — instructing students how to scat, use eighth notes, etc. - and what I find with rhythm is that Europeans tend to put the stress on the downbeat - for example, with

eighth notes...(MH counts off)...and one and two and three and four...instead of one and one and two and three and four... It makes the biggest difference.

Q. Do you have a funny story to tell?

A. We were once working at a club with the vocal group 'Jon Hendricks &Company', and there was this power cut - all the electrical equipment, like the lights, microphones, sound system, etc, went dead. So they lit candles and so we just finished the show a cappella, with the drummer playing his brushes very quietly. Our voices were super soft, but it worked fine; you could hear a pin drop in the club. It was such a unique performance, and so different from the big band sound we're so used to using.

Top photo (left to right) Jon Hendricks & Family: Judth, Michele, Jon, Eric.

Jon Hendricks.

"But you was Bop when you got here, flyin' with the human headed soul Ba, Bird, the doped up revolutionary. Next, you was Cool. It was like your creation yet, of course, very Presidential. Then you got with Philly and them for the harder Bop and then you got Ball, the Dis Heah and Dat Dere of we funky story. Then you sic'ed the straight out vision monster on us, Trane, in the perfect wonderful all-time classical hydrogen bomb and switch blade band. Let us always be able to hear "Straight No Chaser" anytime we want to...."

Excerpt from When Miles Split - 09 / 21 / 1999

NTOZAKE SHANGE

lady in blue

ola
my papa thot he was puerto rican & we wda been
cept we waz just reglar niggahs wit hints of spanish
so off i made it to this 36 hour marathon dance
con salsa con ricardo
'suggggggggar' ray on southern blvd....

TRACIE MORRIS

Give him some
flat-flipped
palm-side
with a dip
the quick-trip
wrist-dip
on the
sleight-of-hand tip....

Notizake Shange: Excerpt from For Colored Girls Who Have Considered Suicide When the Rainbow Is Enuf (Collier Books 1976)

Tracie Morris: Excerpt from Skin in Chap-T-Her Won (TM Ink. 1993)

QUINCY TROUPE and STEVE CANNON poets

QUINCY TROUPE

the assonance of sound breaking from ground
breaking away from itself & found in the bounding syllables of snow
moving now   beginning to roar above the cracking

                                        separation

    crack   crack   caaa-racking   rocks   breaking

way from themselves   a movement   as if raising rock
hands skyward in prayer toward the creator
   is a breaking away of syllables   a breaking & tumbling and shattering...

STEVE CANNON

My creative process in writing to music involves sentence structure, the way I hear the language in terms of the sounds of Afro American speech - I'm more concerned with sound than meaning. And, usually, when I'm called upon to perform with musicians, they'll just break into a Blues mode and I'll improvise along with them in terms of sound: I never know what I'm going to recite or say at a performance until I'm actually there and check out the mood of the place; in other words, there's no script.

Q. Can you describe your interaction with musicians when you're reciting your poetry?

A. Well, I'll tell you something funny that happened. I was performing at Context 2 Music with Jameel Moondoc's Big Band and William Parker, and during the reading, everyone of the musicians stopped playing because they were laughing so hard at the lines I was reciting; when it came time for them to begin playing, they couldn't put the horns to their mouths 'cause they were too busy laughing.

Steve Cannon.

Excerpt from The Sound, Breaking in Avalanche, Poems by Quincy Troupe, Art by Jose Bedila (Coffee House Press, Minneapolis 1996)

The Jazz Gallery
An International Jazz Art Museum
290 Hudson Street, NYC 10013

To Honor Don Pullen: From Gospel to the Glob

Photo Credit: Linda Vartoogian

Remembering Lester

SAINT PETER'S CHURCH
619 Lexington Ave
New York, NY 10022

November 12, 1999
11 o'clock AM

Exhibition and Performance Series
August 24 thru November 21, 1999

Fred Hopkins Memorial Concert

"The George Adams/Don Pullen Quartet were working at Sweet Basil's one night. I came in the door and, to my right, Fred Hopkins was fooling around with Don at the bar. When Fred saw me, he said, "'Hey, Andrew, you wanna sit in, you wanna sit in?" I said, "Man, I just walked in!" But Fred repeated his invitation, "You wanna sit in?" and I said, "Well..." Fred interrupted and said, "Great! I mean on piano, you know!" Andrew Cyrille

"Not many people, except musicians, know what it's like playing a tour that takes you up into Scandinavia. Like Finland, where you play a gig one night, then take a flight over the mountain to get to the next gig. Well, I remember one time, as we were getting ready for one of those flights, and the bus was waiting out in front of the hotel to take us to the airport. Everybody on the tour, including the pilot and crew, was still in the hotel, except for Don Pullen who had gotten his things together and was waiting out in the bus. He was getting nervous because the plane was scheduled to leave at a certain time, and we were late getting started. Only, it didn't matter, because the crew from the plane was inside the hotel with us. Don was the only one who didn't know that, and by the time we came out and got on the bus, he had worked himself up into a near rage. It took quite a while before he calmed down, even after he understood that nobody was going anywhere without the pilot."

- Hamiet Bluiett

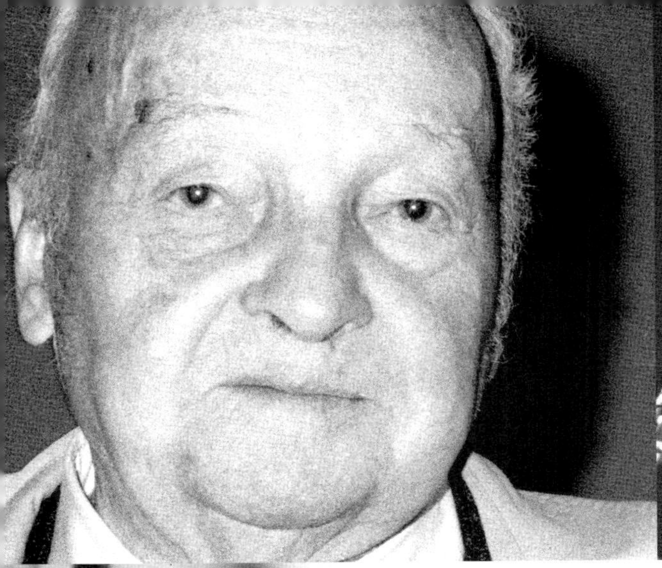

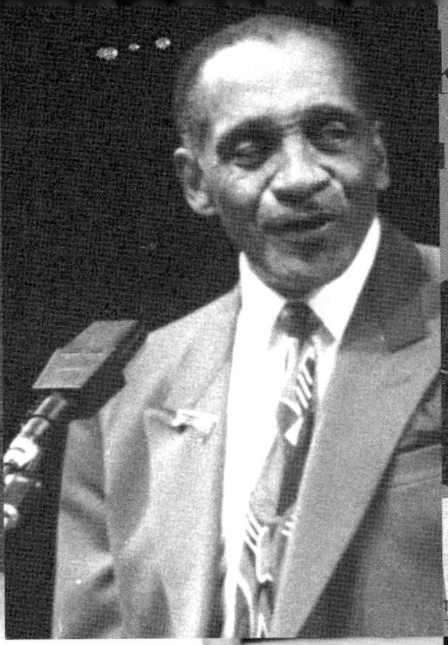

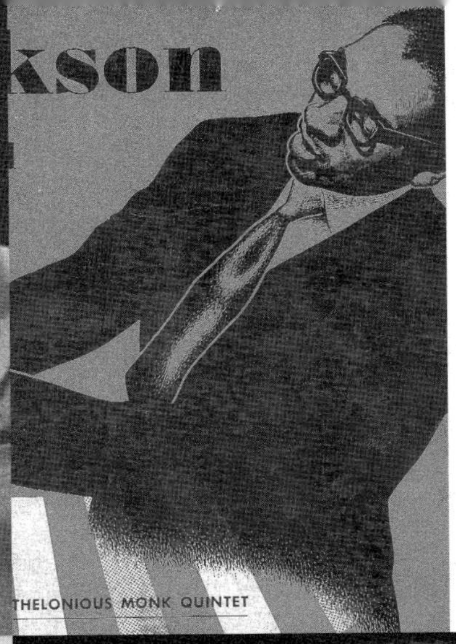

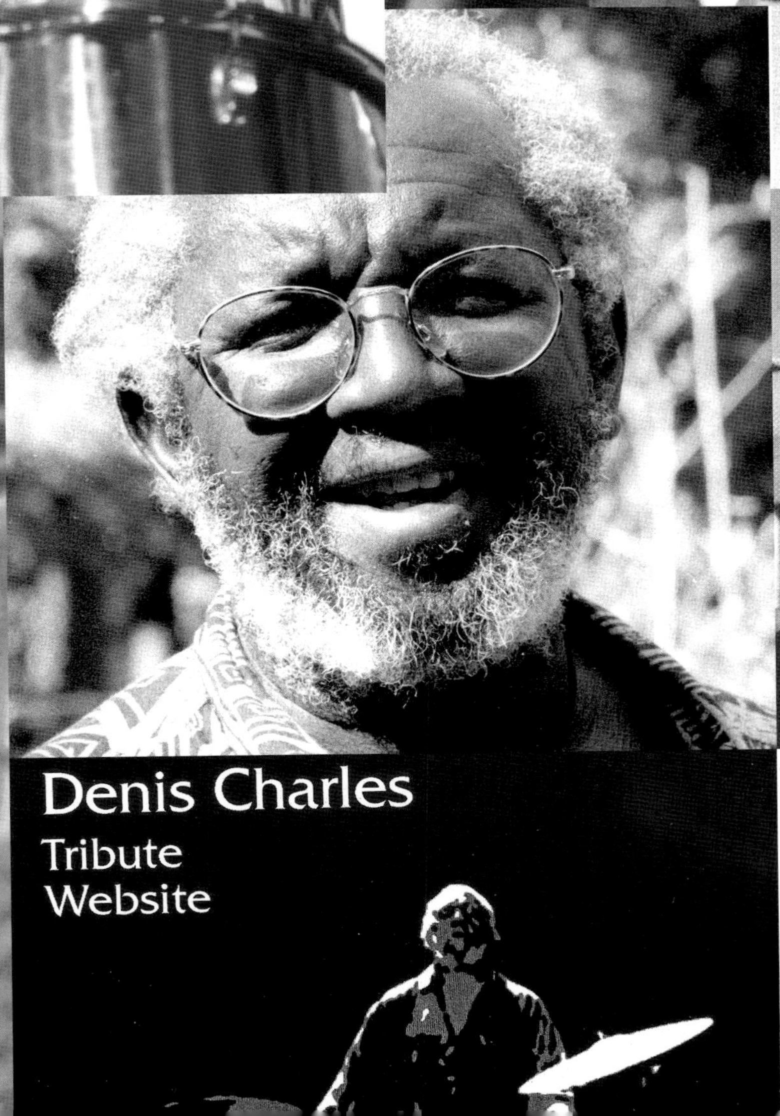

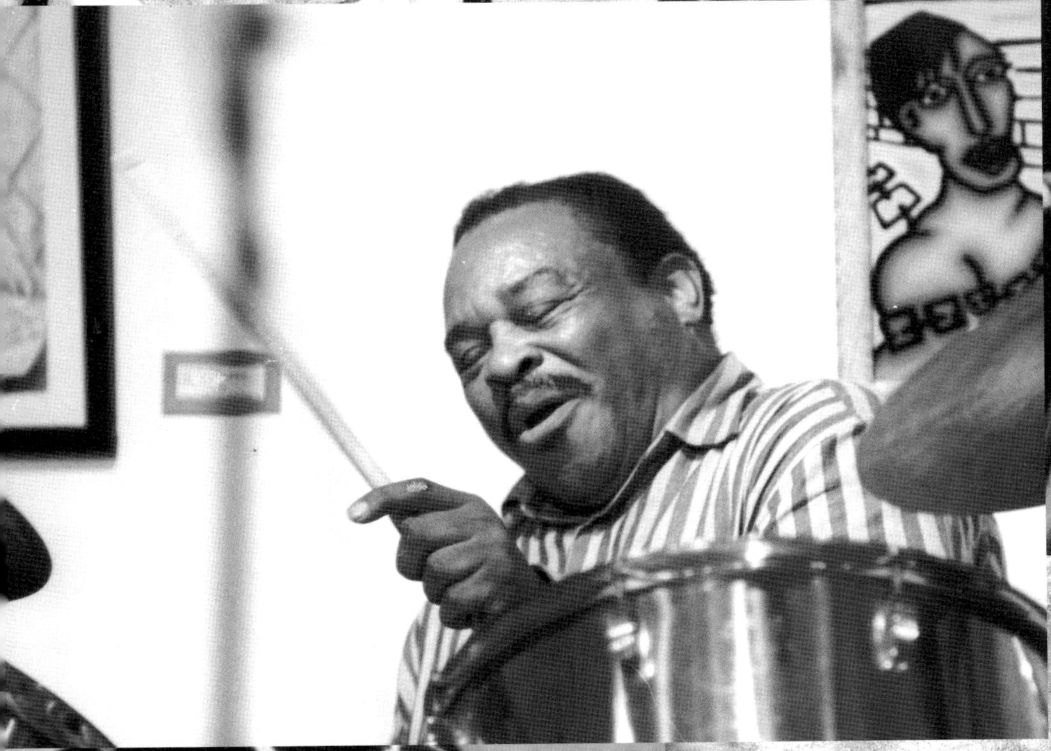

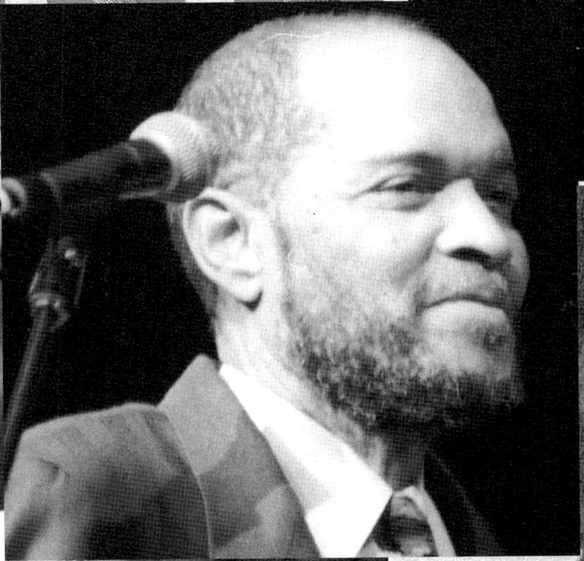

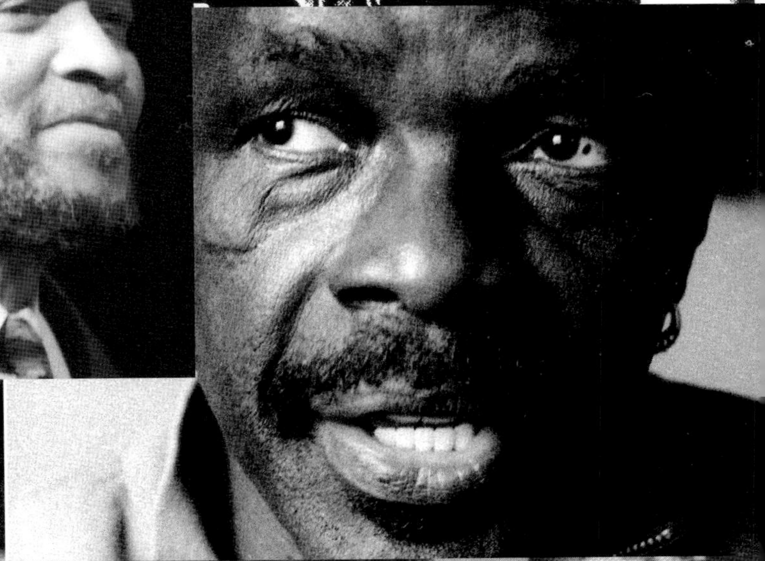

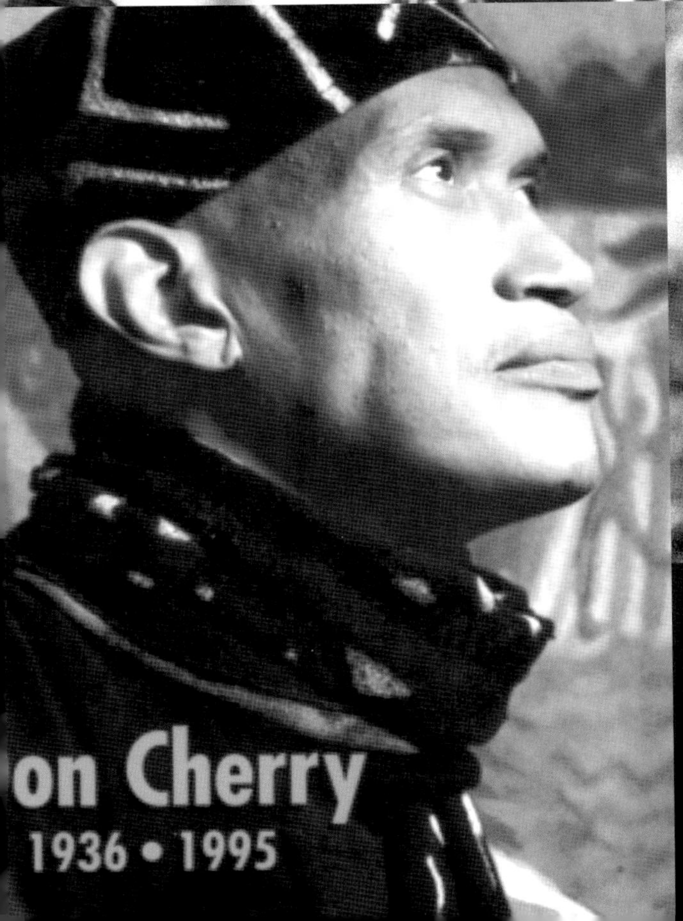

THELONIOUS MONK QUINTET

"For Billy...with Love"
A TRIBUTE AND FUNDRAISER FOR
BILLY HIGGINS
SATURDAY
Nov. 9,
1996
8PM
featuring
PAT METHENY
CHARLIE HADEN
CHARLES LLOYD
GERI ALLEN
RON CARTER
LEWIS NASH
DAVID MURRAY QUARTET
w/JAMES SPAULDING
WILBER MORRIS
MARK JOHNSON
HOWARD JOHNSON
& GRAVITY
SHIRLEY HORN TRIO
w/CHARLES ABLES
STEVE WILLIAMS
CEDAR WALTON TRIO
w/DAVID WILLIAMS
KENNY WASHINGTON
Special Guests
MILT JACKSON
JACKIE McLEAN
CHRIS ANDERSON

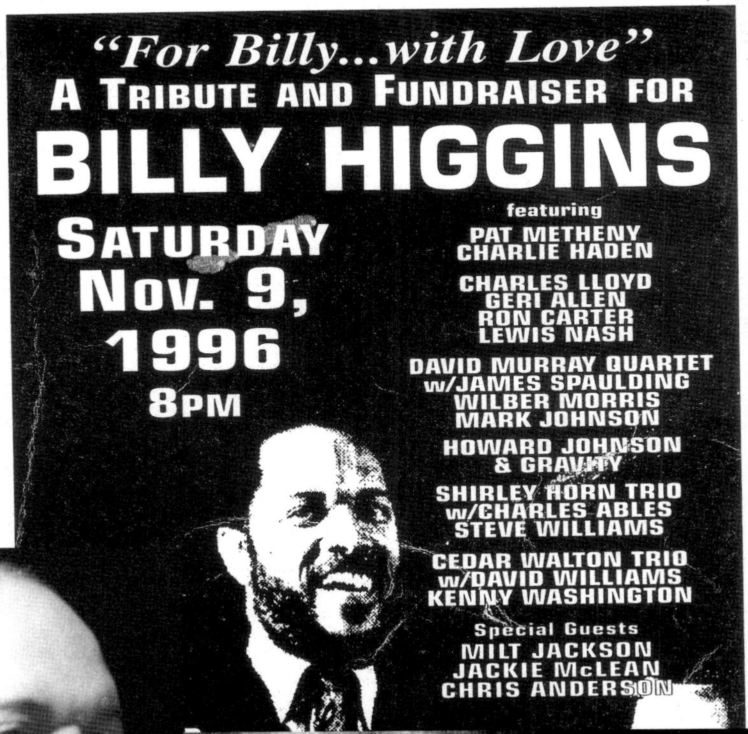

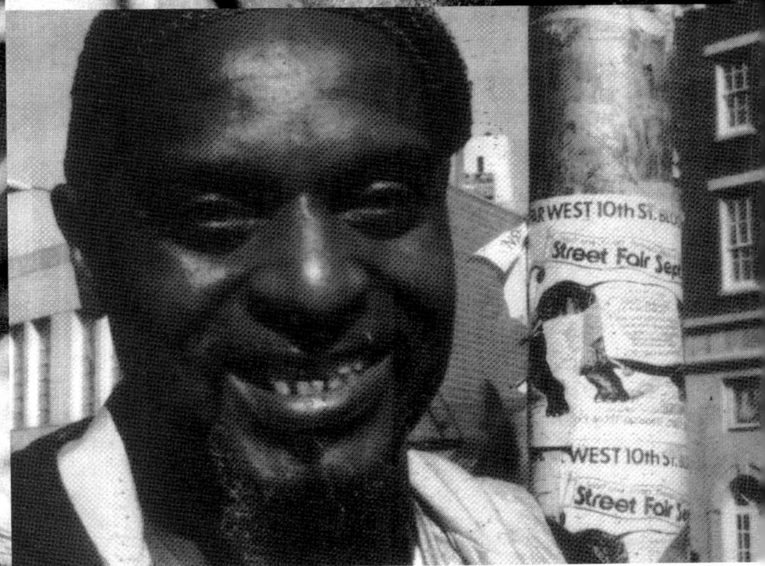

on Cherry
1936 • 1995

Denis Charles
Tribute
Website

WEST 10th St.
Street Fair
WEST 10th St.
Street Fair

Top (left to right) - Maurice Cullaz aka. "Smoothie", Milt Jackson, Billy Higgins.
Center (left to right) - Charles Moffett, Billy Higgins, Makanda Ken McIntyre.
Bottom (left to right) - Don Cherry, Denis Charles, Sulieman el-Hadi.

Julius Hemphill.

Drawing by Jerome Lagarrigue.

(left to right) - David Murray, Arthur Blythe, Oliver Lake, Hamiet Bluiett 1991.

Cadenza

JOE: African American music is a planetary life force. The interviews in this book are witness to an intense musical activity that scuttles the lesser spiritual forms and neutralizes the economic pitfalls endemic to the profession; most of these musicians know what it's like living on the edge. The pages of Jazz Zoom open a window out onto an avant garde underground, successor to the sixties' pioneers, that carries John Coltrane's legacy on and continues to reinvent the music. Musicians who came up in the 70's join forces with the likes of Rashied Ali and Leroy Jenkins, labels like Sound @ One and Aum Fidelity supplant ESP and India Navigation, David Murray helps foment a Big Band revival, and the Arkestra perpetuates the works of its founder's explorations of Pharaoh's Egypt and outer space. The music scene presented here depicts a crucible of lives and experiences that interact continually: the reader gets the impression, upon seeing and listening to the musicians, that an extended family is functioning; the groups reconfigure according to the tenor of works-in-progress and affinities, all of which serves to propel the music forward. The words of Archie Shepp, William Parker or David Murray paint a picture of the networks as well as the essence of this Great Black Music which, at the approach of the millennium, remains vital, creative and inspiring.

Joseph Ghosn, Writer

LECTED DISCOGRAPHY in order of appearance

ge

Albert Ayler: Nuits de la Fondation Maeght (Shandar); Albert Ayler, The Dedication Series, Volumes 1-7 (Impulse); Vibrations and Witches & Devils (Harmonia Mundi)

6. Art Ensemble of Chicago. Full Force (ECM Records GmbH); Coming Home Jamaica (Atlantic Records); Art Ensemble and Lester Bowie's Brass Fantasy: Tokyo Music Joy (DIW Records).

6. Lester Bowie: The Fifth Power, Out Here Like This, Duet - (Black Saint); Brass Fantasy, Avant Pop - (ECM Records, GmbH, Germany).

10. Leroy Jenkins: Leroy Jenkins Live, Urban Blues (Leroy Jenkins' Sting), Lifelong Ambitions (with Muhal Richard Abrams) - (Black Saint).

2. Anthony Braxton: Composition No. 173, Eugene (Northwest Creative Orchestra), Birth and Rebirth (Max Roach), 1-0QA+19 (Muhal Richard Abrams Quintet) - (Black Saint); mposition 102 (Braxton House);

4. Warren Smith. Cats Are Stealing My Shit - (Mapleshade, 2301 Crain Highway, Upper Marlboro, MD. 20772); Studio WIS 20th Anniversary Concert - (Studio Wis Records).

6. Henry Threadgill: Henry Threadgill & Make a Move: Where's Your Cup (Sony Music); Carry The Day (Columbia). Very Very Circus: Spirit of Nuff...Nuff - (Black Saint).

7. Anthony Davis: X: The Life and Times of Malcolm X (An Opera in Three Acts) (Gramavision); Episteme (Gramavision).

8. Fontella Bass: Martha Bass/Fontella Bass/David Peaston/Amina Claudine Myers/Malachi Favors/Philip Wilson: From the Root to the Source (Soul Note); World Saxophone Quartet: reath of Life (Electra/Nonesuch).

20. Frank Gordon. Leroy Jenkins: Themes and Improvisations on the Blues (CRI)

21. Eddie Allen. Remembrance (Venus Records 1994); Rhythm and Blues (Enja 1995); Another Point of View (Enja).

22. Alex Harding: Free Flow (Alex Harding, Jimmy Weinstein, Chris Dahlgren) (CIMP); Bluiett's Baritone Group: Libation for the Baritone Nation (Knitting Factory Records).

22. Aaron Stewart: Your Life Flashes:Vijay Iyer, Elliot Humberto Kavee, Aaron Stewart (Fieldworks); Muhal Richard Abrams: Song For All (Black Saint).

25. John Purcell. World Saxophone Quartet: Taking It 2 The Next Level - (Justin Times Records)

26. Oliver Lake. World Saxophone Quartet: WSQ, Live in Zurich (Black Saint); Oliver Lake Quintet: Dedicated to Dolphy, Expandable Language, Prophet (Black Saint).

28. Hamiet Bluiett. World Saxophone Quartet: Steppin' with the WSQ, Revue (Black Sinat); Hamiet Bluiett Quintet: Dangerously Sweet, Nali Kola (Black Saint). Hamiet Bluiett Sextet: luiett's Barbecue Band - (Mapleshade). .

30. Ronnie Burrage. Natural Burrage (Gema/West Wind); Bluiett's Baritone Saxophone Group: Live At the Knitting Factory - (Knitting Factory Works)

31. Pheeroan akLaff. Global Mantras (Modern Masters); New Air: Air Show #1 (Black Saint).

32. Carol Amber:

32. Donal Fox: Ugly Beauty (Evidence); Gone City (New World Records)

33. Michele Rosewoman: Guardians of the Light and Quintessence (Enja); Spirit (Blue Note).

34. Randy Weston. Randy Weston African Rhythms: Saga; Khepera, Marrakech in the Cool of the Evening, (Verse/Gitanes). David Murray/Randy Weston: The Healers (Black Saint); frican Cookbook (Atlantic).

36. Sun Ra. Sun Ra Arkestra: Reflections in Blue, Hours After, Mayan Temples; Solo Piano: Saint Louis Blues, A tribute to Stuff Smith (Billy Bang/Sun Ra/John Ore/Andrew Cyrille) - Soul Note). Destination Unknown - (Enja Records). Strange Celestial Roads (Rounder Records). Calling Planet Earth - (On Da Music).

38. Marshall Allen. Mark-n-Marshall: Tuesday (Creative Improvised Music Projects); The Sun Ra Arkestra under the direction of Marshall Allen: A Song for the Sun (El Ra Records).

39. Vincent Chancey. Next Mode - (DIW Records); Welcome Mr. Chancey - (IOR).

40. Craig Harris. Craig Harris Quintet: Black Bone, F-Stops (with Hamiet Bluiett) - (Soul Note); Craig Harris and Tailgaters Tales (Shelter).

41. Dick Griffin: The Eighth Wonder & More (Konnex KCD 5059)

42. Jaribu Shahid: David Murray's Octet Plays Trane (Justin Time); James Carter: J.C. On the Set (DIW).

42. Ahmed Abdullah. The Solomonic Quintet (featuring Charles Moffett) and Liquid Magic (Silkheart Records);

Sun Ra Arkestra: Live at Pit-Inn, Tokyo Japan (Evidence) and Destination Unknown (Enja).

44. Billy Bang. Billy Bang Sextet: Live at Carlos 1; Billy Bang Quintet: Valve No. 10; Billy Bang Quartet: Rainbow Gladiator (Soul Note). Bang On - (Justin Time Records).

46. Marion Brown. Marion Brown Quintet: Offering, Mirante do Vale, Offering II - (Venus Records); Porto Novo (Black Lion Records); Back to Paris (featuring Hilton Ruiz) (Harmonia Mundi). Three for Shepp - (Impulse).

48. Fred Hopkins. Air - Air Mail; Diedre Murray/Fred Hopkins: Stringology (Black Saint); Jazz Loft Sessions (Knit Media/Douglas Music); Andrew Cyrille Quintet: My Friend Louis (DIW/Columbia); David Murray Quartet: For Aunt Louise (DIW).

50. Andrew Cyrille. Andrew Cyrille Quintet: Ode to the Living Tree (Evidence Records); Kenny Clarke/ Millford Graves/Famadou Don Moye/Andrew Cyrille: Pieces of Time (Soul Note). Cecil Taylor: Conquistadores, Unit Structures - (Blue Note).

52. Denis Charles. Denis Charles Triangle: Queen Mary (Silkheart); Denis Charles IVTet: Captain of the Deep (Eremite); with Susie Ibarra: Drum Talk (Wobbley Rail); Spirits Gathering (with Billy Bang) - (CIMP).

54. Archie Shepp. California Meeting Live on Broadway, Little Red Moon (Soul Note); The Rising Sun Collection (Justin Time); There's a Trumpet In My Soul (Freedom Records); Fire Music, Mama Too Tight, Attica Blues - (Impulse).

57. Roswell Rudd: Steve Lacy/Roswell Rudd: Trickles (Black Saint); Roswell Rudd/Steve Lacy/ Micha Menhgelberg/Ken Carter/Han Bennik : Regeneration (Soul Note).

58. Reggie Workman. Cerebral Caverns, Summit Conference - (Postcrad Records). Altered Spaces, Synthesis (Leo Records). John Coltrane: The Complete Africa/Brass Sessions, Karma - (Impulse); Archie Shepp: Ballads for Trane - (Denon).

60. Charles Gayle. Consecration (with William Parker) - (Black Saint). Harlem Betrayed, Testaments - (Knitting Factory Works).

61. Rashied Ali. Prima Materia: Peace on Earth, Coltrane's Meditations, Albert Ayler's Bells (Knitting Factory Works); By Any Means (with Charles Gayle & William. Parker): By Any Means (KFW). John Coltrane: Interstellar Space, Meditations - (Impulse).

64. William Parker. William Parker Sextet: In Order to Survive (Black Saint); Touchin' on Trane (FMP Records); Cecil Taylor: Tzotzil Mummers Tzotzil (Leo Records), and Olu Iwa (Soul Note).

66. Susie Ibarra. Susie Ibarra, Assif Tsahar: Home Cookin' (Hopscotch Records)

68. D. D. Jackson. Sigamé, Paired Down, Volumes One and Two (Justin Time); Anthem (BMG)

70. David Murray. David Murray Big Band: Live at Sweet Basil's, Volumes 1 and 2;, Home; David Murray Octet: Hope Scope, Ming (Black Saint); David Murray Quartet: Shakill's Warrior (DIW); Dark Star: The Music of the Grateful Dead (Astor Place Records).

74. Lawrence Butch Morris. Dust to Dust, Testament: A Conduction Collection, No. 11, 15, 22, 23, 28, 31 - (New World Records). David Murray's Big Band: South of the Border - (DIW Records).

76. John Hicks. In the Mix (Landmark Records). Single Petal of a Rose, (Mapleshade); Keystone - (Milestone Records). John Hicks/Elise Wood, Inc. Luminous (Evidence Records); Rhythm-A-Ning (Candid).

78. Elise Wood. John Hicks Trio with Strings ((Mapleshade);

79. Jorge Sylvestre. MusiCollage - (Postcrad Records).

80. Benny Russell. Proverbs (Airmen Records)

82. Frank Ku-umba Lacy. Tonal Weights and Measures (Tutu Records)

83. Abu Salim. In the Path of the Light - (New Face Records)

84. Brian Smith. World Bass Violin Ensemble: Basically Yours (Black Saint)

85. Tani Tabbal. Roscoe Mitchell Sound Ensemble: Snurdy McGurdey and Her Dancing Shoes (Nessa); Geri Allen: Twylight (Verve); David Murray: Remembrances (DIW); James Carter: Jurassic Classics (DIW).

86. James Spaulding. The Smile of the Snake - (High Note Records, 106 W.71st Street, New York, NY 10023).

87. Will Connell. William Parker & the Little Huey Creative Music Orchestra: Flowers Grow In My Room (Centering Records)

87. Alfred Patterson. Muhal Richard Abrams Orchestra: Blu Blu Blu, and Think All, Focus One (Black Saint)

88. Bob Stewart. Then and Now (Postcard Records); Lester Bowie/Brass Fansty: Serious Fun (DIW)

90. Marshall Sealy. Anthony Braxton: Composition 162: Shala Fears for the Poor (Braxton House); J. J. Johnson: Brass Orchestra (Verve); Max Roach with the New Orchestra of Boston & the So What Brass Quintet (Blue Note)

91. Dorian Parreott. Henry Threadgill/Very Very Circus: Too Much Sugar for a Dime(Axiom)

92. Rasul Siddik. Henry Threadgill: Easily Slip into Another World (RCA); David Murray Octet: Picasso (DIW).

93. Ravi Best. Lester Bowie's Brass Fantasy: When The Spirit Returns (Warner Music France); Sam Rivers' Rivbea All-Star Orchestra: Inspiration (RCA Victor)

94. James Zollar. Roaring with Bird (Naxos Jazz 1997); David Murray: South of the Border (DIW).

95. Hugh Ragin. An Afternoon in Harlem (Justin Time); Anthony Braxton: Composition 98 (Art Hat); David Murray: Speaking in Tongues (Justin Time).

98. James Newton. The African Flower - (Blue Note). Above Is Above All - (Contour Records); Buddy Collette Quintet: Flute Talk, and Andrew Cyrille: X-Man (Soul Note); John Carter Quintet: Night Fire (Black Saint).

99. Ricky Ford. Sextet: Songs for My Mother (Quinter) - balaena (Jazz Friends Productions)

99. Carmen Bradford. With Respect and Finally Yours (Evidence)

100. Regina Carter. Something for Grace (Atlantic); Motor City Moments (Verve); Akua Dixon, Quartet Indigo: Afrika! Afrika! (Savant)

104. Abbey Lincoln. Who Used to Dance, A Turtle's Dream, The World is Falling Down, You Gotta Pay the Band (Verve/Gitanes, France). Abbey Lincoln Sings Billie - (Enja Records). That's Him, It's Magic - (Riverside).

106. Billy Johnson. Abbey Lincoln: Talking to the Sun (Enja); Abraham Burton: The Magician (Enja) Mark Johnson. David Murray Octet: Octet Plays Trane (Justin Time)

108. Sonny Simmons. Quintet: Live in San Francisco 1993, with Horace Tapscott: Among Friends (JFD)

109. Marty Ehrlich. Side by Side and New York Child (Enja); Julius Hemphill Sextet: At Dr. King's Table (New World Records); John Carter: Dance of the Love Ghosts (Gramavision).

109. Michael Attias. Credo (Barakacredo@hotmail.com)

110. William Cepeda. Branching Out and My Roots and Beyond (Blue Jackel)

112. Gary Valente. Slide Ride (Ray Anderson, Craig Harris, Gary Valente, George Lewis - (Hat Art Records 4106 Therwil Switzerland)

113. Frank Lowe. Decision in Paradise, Exotic Heartbreak - (Black Saint/Soul Note). Fresh - (Black Lion). Frank Lowe: Live - (DIW Records)

113. Andrew Lamb. Portrait in the Mist - (Delmark)

114. Makanda Ken McIntyre. Stone Blues, Looking Ahead with Eric Dolphy (Prestige)

115. Cecil Bridgewater. Max Roach: To the Max (Enja); Mean What You Say (Brownstone Records); Muhal Richard Abrams: Hearinga Suite (Black Saint).

118. Jackie McLean. The MacBand, New Soil, Let Freedom Ring - (Blue Note); Rhythm of the Earth (Polydor); McLean's Scene (Prestige).

119. Eric McPherson. Abraham Burton/Eric McPherson Quartet: Cause and Effect (Enja)

120. Victor Jones. Visible Sound Groove (One Voice/Satellites)

121. Earl McIntyre. Mingus Big Band: Que Viva Mingus, Gunslinging Birds (Disques Dreyfus); Lester Bowie's Brass Fantasy: My Way (DIW)

122. Dee Dee Bridgewater. Love and Peace (Verve 1994); Prelude to a Kiss (Philips 1996); Dear Ella and This Is New (Polygram).

123. Michele Hendricks. Keepin' Me Satisfied (Muse Records)

124. Amiri Baraka. Blues People

126. Ntozake Shange. For Colored Girls Who Have Considered Suicide When the Rainbow is Enuf

126. Tracie Morris.

127. Quincy Troupe. The Autobiography of Miles Davis as Told to Quincy Troupe

127. Steve Cannon. Groove, Bang and The Jive around (Theuon 2003)

Publishers

DVC Press in association with Overtime Records, Inc., Peoples' Republic of Brooklyn

© Desdemone Bardin/Estate of Desdemone Bardin New York (USA) and France 2000, 2004

LCCN: 2000463972

ISBN 0-9754812-0-7

Visit us at dvcpress.com

E-mail us at siba@dvcpress.com or jerry@dvcpress.com

Credits

All photos by Desdemone Bardin except:

p. 23 Chuck Stewart – photo of John Coltrane

p. 38 Ramsess – post card of Sun Ra (2002 W. 94th Street, Los Angeles 90047)

p. 43 Raymond Ross – photos on Group poster

p. 129 Linda Vartoogian – photo of Don Pullen on flyer

p. 129 Deborah Bowie – photo of Lester Bowie on flyer

Printer

Printed in China by Palace Press International

Book Design

Ikko Asada

Jazz Zoom Shout Outs

Overseen by Desdemone Bardin, through her passion we made it happen.
Dear Mama, I Love U forever… (RIP January 31, 2001)
To Helio Oiticica, now Desdemone is with you.

James Spady, for all your help and links, Udaman, U family. My main man Maurice "Smoothie" Cullaz (RIP), Vonette and Yanis Cullaz, Greg Tate, Joe Ghosn, Michael Attias, Florent Massot, Ikko Asada, Jerome Lagarrigue & Lillian, Walli & Sam Leff, Don & Beverly Greenberg, Dina Gallula.

George Khal, Lynne & Michael Naso, Saundi Wilson, Get Open, Von Meista Dyer, Guka Evans, Dexter Wimberly & Brüknahm Inc., Achille Talon, Yves Zanzi & Lilliane. Manon & Jaques Renan, Robert "Ptit" Michel (RIP), Françoise, Popaul, Francine & Zoe, Louison & Virginie, Bertrand, Phillipe Broussaud, Julian Beck, Judith Malina, Illion Troya, Tom Walker & the entire Living Theatre Cast Old & New, Danny Dawson, Lygia, Paula & the Pape family, Beltrao Family, Cesiñha Oiticica, Gilles Jacquart, Gisèle Cossard, (Zeca Ligiero and Dandara), Cedric & the Legrand Family, Ken Dewey, Donavin White, Magdi Tiema Françoise Denis-Brégeat, Anne Marie Casteret, Doc. Pascal Rafoni & Robin, Clémence René Bazin.

St. Peter's Church, Vision Jazz Fest., Suliaman/Last Poet (RIP), Abiodun Oyewole, , Prof. Arthur Spears, Fanette Vander, Malvina Krum, Nelly, Chantal, Guy Berger, Guiguitte & L'Université Paris VIII, Daniel Richard, Mattias Winkelman, Matthew Kletter, Bill Brown, James & Richie (355 Clinton Neighbors), Lafayette Inspirational Choir (B'klyn), Richard Greene & The Crown Heights Project, Jazz Hot Magazine, Daily Challenge, WBAI Radio-Bernard White & Amy Goodman, Palace Press, Yazid Manou, Rasul Siddik, KZ, Olivier, Effay & The Vibe (Vincennes).

To the Hospital Staffs:
Dr. Kendall, Dr. Grossman, Dr. Bixon & Long Island Univ. Hospital Doctors, Nurse Martinez (you're a gem). Dr. Smith, Dr. Emond & Columbia Presbyterian Hospital staff.

A Special shout to Leroy Jenkins, D.D. Jackson & Aaron Stewart for the visits during Desdemona's sickness.
To my family (friends) who kept me up after Desdemone's passing…
Kiambu, Saundi, Jerome, Dimitri, Jesse, Cedric, Manu, Guka, Bill, Xiomara, Liz, Brooklyn Conservatory Staff, Joy & Ralph "The Wizard" Sepson (I hope you make it thru…)
And to Papa, Jerry Greenberg, Hey DVC Press is born, Impex is next… then your memoirs…

Peace & Blessings >>> Sebastian "SibaGiba-SBG" Bardin-Greenberg

Hey, now…hey, Desdemone,

On the other side of the sky (Ahhretha). Mars has come over to ours for a spell and I've been watching it most nights working its way to the west and away in these weeks running up to taking Jazz Zoom to the printer. The book may not have come as soon as you wanted but, trust us, it's right in time!

First, thanks go to you. Muhal told me how fortunate SBG and I are that you left us such a treasure, this music history that is about to make the scene.

To James Spady and Ikko Asada whose counsel, enthusiasm and input into the book propelled us at crucial times toward its realization.

To Farhad Farhadi whose technical guidance and mastery of keys opened locked doors and signaled trap doors, Nzingah Oyo and Kiambu Dickerson for their expert photographic eyes, and Grand Army Plaza One Hour Photo Studio, 319 Flatbush Avenue, Peoples' Republic of Brooklyn, 11217 for superb black/white photo printing.

A tes proches: en France en dehors de Paris – Huguette/Gaston/Eric, Manon/Jacques, Marie Laure/Bernard, Fabienne/Pascal, Lassad/Suzie, Cherif, Jeannie et Linette, pour leur acceuil et amour et apport d'eaux…douces (du Loing), salées (de la Méditerrané) et sulphureuses (de source pyrennéenne); et au Québec – la famille Chartrand, Francine/Léandre/Déirdre, George Khal, Christian Allègre.

To Bev/Don; Ken Dewey, my main man; An Chi Ho, you go, girl; Michael Hittman for our first pre-publication radio interview; Michael Attias for his translation skills and musicianship – "Do I hear a bass?"; my teaching colleagues and staff at Long Island University and New York City College of Technology; the Attica Brothers and their steadfast lawyers, Holly Price, Bea "Mail lady" Warren, Tina/Merrick, Trudy/Bruce, Dana Beal, Alice Torbush, Aron Kaye, Bonnie Tocwish, Rob McDonald (RIP), Nestor Z., Scott K., the Thompsons Jean-Rémy/Francis Z.

And to the musicians who've attended what has now become our annual tribute: Leroy, Rashied, Andrew. Reggie, Craig, D.D., Rasul, Benny, Will, Aaron, Ahmed, Alex, Eric McPherson, Abraham Burton, Gwen Laster, Justin Asher, Saundi Wilson, Cecil Young, Marivaldo, Jimi Weinstein, Von Meista and Kiambu, Thierry and Olivier, Karim, and the members of Lafayette Inspirational Ensemble – Janis, Mike, Cie, Allison, Aaron…and I'll stop there except for another nod to Aretha: DVC Press…That's What I Like About Cha.

Amor, saudade, Rio de Janiero

(Excerpt from) Cotton Comes to Harlem by Chester Himes`

Afterwards [Grave Digger and Coffin Ed] sauntered towards the
back and stood beside the bandstand watching the white and
black couples dancing the twist in the cabaret. The horns were
talking and the saxes talking back.

"Listen to that", Grave Digger said when the horn took on a
frenetic solo, "Talking under their clothes, ain't it?"

Then the two saxes started swapping tours with the rhythm
always in the back. "Somewhere in that jungle is the solution
to the wold", Coffin Ed said, "if we could only find it."

 "Yeah, it's like the sidewalks trying to speak in a language never
heard. But they can't spell it either."

"Naw", Coffin Ed said, "unless there's an alphabet for emotion."

"The emotion that comes out of experience. If we could read
that language, man, we would solve all the crimes in the world."

"Let's split", Coffin Ed said, "Jazz talks too much to me."

"It ain't so much what it says", Grave Digger agreed, "It's what
you can't do about it."